BEYOND
THE
FREEZE

BEYOND THE FREEZE

THE ROAD TO NUCLEAR SANITY

Daniel Ford, Henry Kendall, Steven Nadis

THE UNION OF
CONCERNED
SCIENTISTS

Beacon Press   Boston

IN WRITING this book, we have benefited from the technical advice, editorial assistance, and generous help of many people. Those who contributed their time and expertise to our effort include Kurt Gottfried, Nuhad Jamal, Thomas Longstreth, James MacKenzie, Leonard Meeker, Veronika Neudachin, Olga Pastuchiv, Bette Pounders, Howard Ris, Sigmund Roos, Suzanne Stein, Gerald Steinberg, Lois Traub, Eric Van Loon, Paul Walker, and Michael Wyson.

Beacon Press books are published under the auspices
of the Unitarian Universalist Association,
25 Beacon Street, Boston, Massachusetts 02108
Published simultaneously in Canada by
Fitzhenry & Whiteside Limited, Toronto

Printed in the United States of America

(paperback) 9   8   7   6   5   4   3   2   1

Library of Congress Cataloging in Publication Data

Ford, Daniel F.
  Beyond the freeze.
  Includes bibliographical references and index.

  1. Arms control.   2. Atomic weapons and
disarmament.   I. Kendall, Henry Way, 1926–
II. Nadis, Steven J.   III. Union of Concerned
Scientists.   IV. Title.
JX1974.F59   1982   327.1'74   82–72504
ISBN 0–8070–0484–7 (pbk.)

CONTENTS

INTRODUCTION:

NUCLEAR ANGST

"To the village square we must carry the facts of atomic energy. From there must come America's voice."
—*Albert Einstein, 1946*

A GENERATION later, Americans have begun to take the great physicist at his word. In New England town meetings, in petitions signed on California street corners, in churches, universities, and civic groups around the country, concerned citizens are finally facing up to the greatest issue of our age: the threat of an annihilating nuclear war.

For many years, this grim subject was rarely discussed: it was just too depressing to think about. During the "me decade" of the seventies, the topic was far from the worrisome one it had been in the 1950s and early 1960s when fallout from U.S. and Soviet atmospheric testing of nuclear weapons reminded people of the danger. After the 1963 treaty banning such tests, public concern abated. For the next several years, with the Vietnam war and all of the nation's other difficulties, the issue receded further from public consciousness.

Still, in the past two years, we have been jolted into recognizing that nuclear war is far more likely than many Americans had believed.

During the 1980 presidential campaign candidate Ronald

Reagan delivered a dire warning. Because of the unrelenting Soviet nuclear buildup of the preceding decade, he declared, the United States was becoming dangerously exposed to a Russian surprise attack. We suffered, he said, from a "window of vulnerability," a weakness in our ability to deter the Soviet Union from starting a nuclear war. His campaign platform called for an aggressive program to achieve nuclear "superiority" over the U.S.S.R.

Once in office, Mr. Reagan promptly initiated the largest U.S. military buildup ever undertaken in peacetime. Included in the program was a massive expansion of the U.S. nuclear arsenal. What is more, the President casually announced—in response to a reporter's question—that nuclear weapons could actually be *used* to fight a "limited" nuclear war. Alexander Haig, Secretary of State at the time, spoke similarly of using "demonstration" nuclear blasts during a crisis to show the Soviets our resolve.

Intended to frighten the Russians, the new administration's program also frightened the American and European public. In Western Europe, mass demonstrations were held to protest the planned deployment, which our NATO allies had requested, of new U.S. nuclear missiles on the continent. In the United States, a grassroots protest began, and it has grown quickly, and unexpectedly, into a mass movement challenging the official plans for an open-ended arms race with the Soviet Union.

Opponents of the current U.S. defense program have been doing more than criticizing specific weapons systems. They have been discussing far-reaching proposals for ending the nuclear arms race once and for all.

One of the most popular ideas is a bilateral nuclear arms "freeze." The freeze is not the usual kind of "arms control" proposal. It is not a draft treaty, full of complex, carefully worded provisions. It is not the kind of detailed prescription for regulating the arms race that technical experts, State Department officials, or other professionals might draft.

The freeze is a simple, unadorned, and seemingly uncomplicated notion: the United States and the Soviet Union should agree to a dead halt in all aspects of the nuclear arms race. Both sides, that is, should stop the buildup and testing of nuclear bombs and the delivery systems that bring them to their targets.

- Does such a proposal make sense? Is stopping the arms race really as easy as that?
- Or is the freeze just simplistic, wishful thinking?
- Will the proposal "freeze the United States into a position of military disadvantage and dangerous vulnerability," as the Reagan administration claims?
- Or is it the essential "first step" to halt the nuclear arms race, as advocates contend?
- If it is just the first step, what are the next ones that will have to be taken to reduce the risks of nuclear war?
- Should the United States and Soviet Union make drastic cuts in the size of their present nuclear arsenals?
- Will a declaration that the United States and its allies will never be the first to use nuclear weapons, following the lead of the Soviet Union, help improve our security?
- Can improved nonnuclear military defenses reduce the risk of a confrontation in Europe that could trigger World War III?

This book tries to answer these questions. Before you take down a fence, Robert Frost counseled, you should know why it was put up. In trying to curb the nuclear arms race, it would be useful to understand something of its history and the forces that drive it forward. The purpose of this book, accordingly, is to provide a simple primer on the basic issues involved in the current debate and to outline steps necessary to reduce, and hopefully eliminate, the threat of nuclear war.

Part I looks at the key developments that have led to the present level of nuclear arms. Part II analyzes the feverish new buildup of nuclear weaponry planned by the United States. Part III reviews the pros and cons of the freeze proposal and describes other, broader measures that can help avoid the ultimate calamity of nuclear war.

PART I

THE NUCLEAR ARMS RACE

1

A WARNING

"It's a damn shame you can't feel safe in Damascus, Arkansas—a little bitty place nobody in the country heard of before yesterday."

—Damascus resident,
September 20, 1980

KITTY'S RESTAURANT in Bee Branch, Arkansas (population 62), is one of the places where people have begun to talk about the problem of nuclear war.

"I'm no nuclear physicist," Kitty Murdock, the owner, said, "but I'm smart enough to ask some questions."

Kitty and other local residents had good reason to raise questions. On September 19, 1980, a U.S. Air Force Titan II missile, based a few miles up the highway to Damascus, accidentally exploded. Its fuel leaked and caught fire. The nuclear warhead was ejected from the missile but didn't go off.

The nearby population, forced to leave their homes in the middle of the night, got the fright of their lives. They also started thinking about the eighteen other Air Force Titan II missiles housed in their midst.

"We're surrounded," said a farmer from Damascus. "Until the accident, people just hadn't been aware of how heavily armed the state is. Now I know that if there was a nuclear war, I'd be the target."

Before the accident, the missile silos had been accepted unquestioningly. "I never thought much about those things before," said a county government worker. "They just seemed like big orange turtlebacks lying quiet on the ground with a lot of antennas."

Local apathy quickly turned to rage. "We want the blooming things moved out!" shouted a middle-aged woman outside the Methodist Church in Damascus on the Sunday morning after the accident. "We want the missile base so far away that it would take a dollar to send a postcard to it," another resident added.

The big concern among the farmers who were the regulars at Kitty's Restaurant had been the summer of punishing drought there in the foothills of the Ozarks. But regional newspapers after the explosion devoted more space to "megatons" and "radioactivity" than to the weather. Readers and television watchers were given a crash course on the facts of life in a nuclear-armed world.

Kitty was particularly surprised by a fact she gleaned from the local newspapers: the Titan II missile carried a nine-megaton hydrogen bomb. A megaton is the explosive power of a million tons of TNT. The bomb on the Titan II, the newspaper noted, was seven hundred times as powerful as the Hiroshima bomb, which killed more than one hundred thousand people.

"I wasn't aware before that they were so big," Kitty said in amazement.

When she learned that the United States had thousands of atomic bombs far more powerful than the one dropped on Hiroshima, Kitty became annoyed about all the money that was being spent on these weapons. "I really work very hard for my money," she said. "The people around here work real hard. I don't like this money being squandered."

"I don't want Russia to take over," she added. "We should defend our country. But do we need these missiles seven hundred times as big as Hiroshima? How many times do we need to kill the Russians? It seems like we're going after an ant with a baseball bat. Why do we have to do that when a fly swatter will do just as well?"

2

THE
BALANCE SHEET

*"The number of tactical nuclear weapons? . . . I'll connect
you with one of our bean-counting specialists."*
                                        —Receptionist,
                                        Center for Defense
                                        Information, 1982

KITTY'S THINKING is becoming more and more common.
Like most Americans, she appreciates the threat to the United
States (and other nations) posed by the U.S.S.R.: a dangerous,
overmilitarized society with interests antithetical to our own.

With the vast U.S. arsenal of nuclear weapons, however,
many people think we already have enough—indeed, more than
enough—nuclear bombs to deter any Soviet attack on this country and its allies. How could the U.S.S.R. ever consider an attack
if we are able to counterattack with such devastating force?

Other people, nevertheless, worry that our nuclear forces
are not up to snuff, and may in fact be "inferior" to those of the
Soviet Union.

An honest accounting of the size and power of U.S. and
Soviet nuclear arsenals is needed to resolve this basic difference
of opinion.

Because the weapons of the United States and Soviet Union
come in different types and sizes and have varying technical fea-

tures, we must do more than simply count the number of bombs each possesses. What is needed to assess each side's nuclear arsenal is some yardstick that accurately conveys its overall military significance.

The experts usually talk of nuclear bombs in terms of their explosive force measured in "megatons" or in "equivalent-megatons" to account for the way that blast damage varies with bomb size. They also talk about the "throw weight" of each missile (the weight of the nuclear warheads they are able to carry). Such abstract terms surely fail to describe the full effects of these bombs: the lives they would take, the cities they would destroy, the industrial capacity they would eliminate.

A simple, understandable benchmark for summarizing the power of a given nuclear weapon is to define its explosive power relative to the bomb dropped on Hiroshima. Let us say, then, that such and such a bomb is a 10-Hiroshima bomb or a 50-Hiroshima bomb, rather than using the military jargon. (Such a measure of relative destructiveness is only a rough approximation, of course, since all the effects of a bomb do not increase in strict proportion to its yield.) The U.S. Air Force refers to the warhead on a Titan II missile as a 9-megaton bomb. In tallying U.S. nuclear forces, we will count it simply as a 700-Hiroshima bomb. (This one bomb, remarkably, carries greater explosive force than all the bombs dropped by all sides during World War II.) The Soviets have a long-range bomber known as the *"Bear."* It carries a 20-megaton bomb; we'll put it down in our accounting book as a 1,600-Hiroshima bomb.

U.S. NUCLEAR STRENGTH

The superpowers' nuclear balance sheet can be straightforwardly assembled. First, on one side, we can tabulate the "strategic" nuclear forces of the United States. These are the bombs that can be launched against targets in the Soviet heartland. There are several means of doing so: first, land-based intercontinental ballistic missiles—ICBMs, for short; second, nuclear submarines hidden in the oceans and equipped with long-range ballistic missiles; third, both manned bombers and unmanned drone aircraft designed to penetrate Soviet air defenses.

The mainstay of the U.S. ICBM force is 1,000 Minuteman missiles, each of which carries 1 to 3 nuclear bombs ranging from 14 to 120 Hiroshimas in size. Altogether, our Minuteman force can deliver 2,100 nuclear bombs to the Soviet heartland. (The United States also has 52 of the older, but larger, Titan missiles carrying single warheads.) The total potential of U.S. ICBMs: devastation equivalent to over 120,000 Hiroshimas.

The ICBM force, although awesome, actually carries fewer bombs than the other two legs of our strategic "triad." Our submarine-launched ballistic missiles—of which we have some 520—and our 350 long-range bombers each carry a bigger share of the U.S. strategic arsenal.

Examining the capabilities of a single nuclear submarine reveals its incredible destructive potential. A Poseidon sub comes equipped with 16 missiles. Each missile can carry 10 or more warheads, each equivalent to 3 Hiroshima bombs, that can be directed to separate targets. (The Poseidon subs that have been retro-fitted with newer Trident I missiles have even more powerful warheads.) Altogether, the 160 bombs on a single Poseidon can drop the equivalent of more than 500 Hiroshimas on the Soviet Union. A single sub would therefore be capable of simultaneously attacking such Soviet cities as Moscow, Leningrad, Kiev, Tashkent, Baku, Kharkov, Gorky, Novosibirsk, Kuibyshev, and Sverdlovsk—each having a population in excess of a million—and *still* have at least 150 warheads available to wipe out other cities, villages, and hamlets. This is the power of just one Poseidon sub, of which the United States has thirty-one.

The full potential of the strategic "triad" of ICBMs, subs, and bombers being developed by the United States in the 1960s was described by an Assistant Secretary of Defense: "First we need enough Minutemen to be sure that we destroy all those Russian cities. Then we need the Polaris missiles to follow in order to tear up the foundations to a depth of ten feet . . . Then, when all Russia is silent, and no air defenses are left, we want waves of aircraft to drop enough bombs to tear the whole place up down to a depth of forty feet to prevent the Martians recolonizing the country. And to hell with the fallout."

All told, the United States has some 9,500 bombs in its strategic nuclear arsenal. Their average strength—the standard, off-the-shelf piece of U.S. nuclear ordnance—is about 30 times the power of the Hiroshima bomb.

But this is not the end of the story. In addition to these gigantic "strategic" weapons, we also have "tactical" bombs— some less than one-twentieth the size of the Hiroshima bomb, but others larger than Poseidon warheads. Intended for "battlefield" or "theater" use against nearby targets, these include the bombs loaded in short- and intermediate-range missiles, artillery launchers, howitzers, and land mines.

The stockpile of U.S. nuclear weapons, of all sizes, contains, all told, some 25,000 to 30,000 bombs.

SOVIET NUCLEAR STRENGTH

The Soviet Union has a correspondingly awesome nuclear arsenal. They have approximately 7,800 strategic warheads that could unleash the equivalent of about 360,000 Hiroshimas on the United States. With 25 percent of the U.S. population concentrated in ten metropolitan areas, the Soviets could wreak massive destruction with only a few dozen bombs—barely making a dent in their strategic arsenal.

The largest component of the Soviet arsenal is its land-based missiles. The Soviet Union has been steadily modernizing its ICBM force, replacing older missiles with the more modern SS–17s, SS–18s, and SS–19s. The new missiles, equipped with multiple warheads, now comprise over half the total. The largest Soviet missile, the SS–18, has a range of over 6,000 miles. It can carry up to 10 warheads, each about 50 Hiroshimas in size.

All told, the Soviets have about 1,400 ICBMs, which can deliver 5,500 nuclear bombs to American soil. Each of these bombs has the equivalent power of about 50 Hiroshimas.

The Soviet fleet of 62 submarines carries 950 missiles armed with 1,900 nuclear bombs ranging from 16 to 80 Hiroshimas in size. In 1980, the Soviets launched the *Typhoon,* a new submarine much larger than its predecessors. Equipped with 20 long-range ballistic missiles, each armed with 12 warheads, this submarine will be able to threaten 240 American cities.

The 150 Soviet long-range bombers carry an estimated 400 nuclear bombs with an average yield of about 80 Hiroshimas.

Since 1977, the Soviet Union has deployed about 250 mobile SS–20 missiles. These intermediate-range weapons, along with their strategic weapons and tactical bombs available for use in Europe and Asia, add up to a total Soviet inventory of about 20,000 bombs.

Together, the United States and the Soviet Union have accumulated 45,000 to 50,000 nuclear bombs with a total destructive force of about a million Hiroshimas—6,000 pounds of TNT for every person in the world.

"Who is ahead in the arms race?" many people ask. "The Americans or the Russians?"

Answering this question is like comparing the overstuffed investment portfolios of two billionaires who hold their assets in different forms and trying to determine who is richer. The United States and Soviet Union have chosen to assemble different kinds of nuclear arsenals, so summing up their overall military capabilities is not simply a matter of "counting beans."

For example, if the total number of delivery vehicles—ICBMs, submarine missiles, and bombers—is the standard, the Soviets are ahead by about 2,500 to 1,900.

Of course, the number of bombs carried by the various delivery vehicles is also an important factor in determining the relative nuclear firepower of the two countries. If the total number of strategic nuclear bombs is the standard, then the United States is ahead 9,500 to 7,800. (We piggyback more warheads on each missile than the Russians do.)

Soviet bombs are larger than ours, however. They can make *bigger* craters than we can, but we can make *more* craters than they can.

The Soviets have elected to place the bulk of their weaponry in heavy land-based missiles carrying large blockbuster warheads. They have some 5,500 ICBM warheads to our 2,152.

THE NUCLEAR BALANCE SHEET:
U.S. and Soviet Strategic Nuclear Forces (1982)

	UNITED STATES		
	Delivery Vehicles	*Warheads*	*Approximate Explosive Power in Hiroshima-bomb equivalents*
Intercontinental Ballistic Missiles	1,052	2,152	123,000
Submarine-Launched Ballistic Missiles	520	4,800	23,000
Bombers	350	2,600	130,000
TOTAL	1,922	9,552	276,000

	SOVIET UNION		
	Delivery Vehicles	*Warheads*	*Approximate Explosive Power in Hiroshima-bomb equivalents*
Intercontinental Ballistic Missiles	1,400	5,500	270,000
Submarine-Launched Ballistic Missiles	950	1,900	59,000
Bombers	150	400	33,000
TOTAL	2,500	7,800	362,000

Source: Stockholm International Peace Research Institute, *The Arms Race and Arms Control, 1982;* Center for Defense Information, "U.S.–U.S.S.R. Strategic Nuclear Forces," 1982; *The New York Times,* April 2, 1982.

This does not give them general "nuclear superiority"; it just indicates their preference for a particular type of weapons system. The United States, opting for greater diversity, has chosen smaller, but more accurate, warheads spread more evenly among nuclear submarines, long-range bombers, and land-based missiles. We have about 4,800 sublaunched strategic warheads, for example, and they have only 1,900.

In short, there is no general answer to the question "Who's ahead?" It all depends on the specific category you happen to be looking at.

Certain factors, moreover, can't be put in terms of numbers. U.S. subs, for example, are quieter than theirs, which makes them harder to detect and less vulnerable to attack. They also run much more reliably. The United States keeps 60 percent of its fleet on patrol on a continuous basis; the Soviets only manage to keep 10 percent in the ocean on a regular basis.

Still, the fact that the United States is "ahead" in submarine technology and sublaunched warheads does not translate to an overall nuclear edge.

"We're way ahead" in the number of strategic warheads, former SALT negotiator Paul Warnke says. "It doesn't make a damn bit of difference. In megatonnage, the Soviets are way ahead; it doesn't make a damn bit of difference. The fact that they might have a two-megaton warhead compared to our modest ones of something like 400,000 tons of TNT only makes one difference: How big is the hole going to be where the high school used to be?"

With conventional weapons, the more one side has, the greater its ostensible military advantage. Not always, of course, for David *did* slay Goliath, but the Goliaths can usually count on being able to trounce the Davids.

With nuclear weapons, however, the benefit of having large numbers matters much less. If both sides are already Supergoliaths, with many more than enough weapons to obliterate each other, the military "advantage" of obtaining further weapons becomes meaningless.

"What in the name of God is strategic 'superiority'?" former

Secretary of State Henry Kissinger asked in 1974. "What is the significance of it, politically, militarily, operationally, at these levels of numbers? What do you do with it?"

Both the United States and the Soviet Union have enough nuclear bombs to destroy each other's cities some 50 times over. Accordingly, any "inequality" in the number of bombs they possess "doesn't make a rat's ass bit of difference," a salty U.S. admiral commented recently. The bombs each side continues to build, he noted, provide no *usable* military advantage. Additional warheads merely give the attacker the capacity, as Winston Churchill said, to "make the rubble bounce."

Like billionaires, who have more money than they could ever hope to spend, the United States and the Soviet Union have wildly excessive nuclear strength, more than enough to dissuade each other from starting a nuclear war.

The problem facing strategic planners on both sides is not the lack of nuclear weapons, but a shortage of interesting targets. The United States and the U.S.S.R. would run out of cities and military bases worth destroying long before they ran out of bombs.

3

MUTUAL SUSPICION

"It may seem melodramatic to say that the U.S. and Russia represent Good and Evil, Light and Darkness, God and the Devil. But if we think of it that way, it helps to clarify our perspective of the world struggle."
—Richard Nixon, 1980

THE UNITED STATES and the U.S.S.R., by any reasonable accounting, each have an overabundant supply of nuclear bombs.

Still, they relentlessly build more and more instruments of mass destruction.

How does one explain this frantic—and seemingly pointless —contest? What has driven the superpowers to build such obscenely large nuclear arsenals? What keeps them going?

To understand the momentum behind the nuclear arms race, we must take note of the political, bureaucratic, and technological factors that shaped the cold war that began in the aftermath of World War II as a result of the Soviet Union's subjugation of Eastern Europe.

In 1945, the United States had a monopoly on nuclear technology—a position many American leaders enjoyed and wanted to preserve.

"God almighty in his infinite wisdom [has] dropped the A-bomb in our lap," Senator Edwin Johnson of Colorado said in

November 1945. "With vision and guts and plenty of A-bombs [the United States] could compel mankind to adopt the policy of peace . . . or be burned to a crisp."

U.S. scientists warned, however, that other nations could unravel the mysteries of nuclear fission and develop their own nuclear capability. The specter of more Hiroshimas prompted the Truman administration, for a brief period, to entertain a proposal—called the Acheson-Lilienthal plan—for the international control of nuclear technology. There was also much talk in the immediate postwar years of the need to abandon independent "nation states" and to form a "world government." No longer could traditional international rivalries be tolerated, it was said, now that hostilities could give rise to nuclear confrontations.

Deep-seated mistrust quickly shattered proposals for preventing the spread of nuclear weapons. The Soviet Union summarily rejected the Acheson-Lilienthal plan, thinking it a ruse to preserve the nuclear monopoly so evidently enjoyed by Senator Johnson and several other U.S. leaders.

U.S. military officials, moreover, were anxious to build up America's nuclear arsenal, while preventing the Soviets from acquiring one. "Our monopoly of the bomb, even though it is transitory, may well prove to be a critical factor in our efforts to achieve first a stabilized condition and eventually a lasting peace," Air Force General Carl Spaatz said in June 1946.

"We cannot at this time limit our capability to produce or use this weapon," Army Chief of Staff General Dwight Eisenhower commented the same year.

The United States, under the leadership of the Atomic Energy Commission, moved ahead swiftly to develop and expand its nuclear capability. The official attitude toward the Soviet Union hardened, with President Truman undertaking a campaign, starting in March 1947, to convince the American public, as one of his advisers explained, that "the war isn't over by any means."

The worst fears of the United States were confirmed in September 1949, when the Soviet Union detonated its first atomic bomb. China also "fell" to the Communists that year.

The United States responded to these setbacks with a frantic effort to develop a "super bomb"—the so-called hydrogen bomb or "H-bomb"—which would be hundreds, or perhaps thousands, of times more powerful than the atomic bombs dropped on Japan.

We got the H-bomb in 1952; the Soviet Union, not content to let the United States push ahead unilaterally, tested one in 1953. A full-scale arms race was underway.

Amplifying the contest between the United States and the U.S.S.R. was an ideological battle that made the struggle as much a religious war as a military competition.

"My own theory about Communism," evangelist Billy Graham said in the 1950s, "is that it is masterminded by Satan. I think there is no other explanation for the tremendous gains of Communism in which they seem to outwit us at every turn, unless they have supernatural power."

"This political force," U.S. Ambassador to the Soviet Union George Kennan wrote in 1946, "is seemingly inaccessible to considerations of reality in its basic reactions."

"I think it is a mistake to believe that you can at any time sit down with the Russians and solve questions," Undersecretary of State Dean Acheson commented in 1947.

Fueled by such strong sentiments—on both sides—a full-scale nuclear arms race took root. It proved over the following quarter-century to have an ineradicable, weedlike vitality.

4

THE CAUCUS RACE

"SENATOR BROOKE: *What I am getting at, Admiral, is, as we improve our capability, then the Soviets respond by trying to catch up with us; and as they begin to catch up with us, we find it necessary to improve our capability beyond that. I am just wondering where this ends.*
"ADMIRAL MOORER: *Well, I think it is a function of technology, Senator, and I do not think it ever ends. I mean, this has been going on since the stone age.*"
—*U.S. Senate Hearing, 1969*

U.S. AND SOVIET leaders fired repeated rhetorical salvos at each other as the cold war heated up.

Secretary of State John Foster Dulles, following his policy of "brinkmanship," warned that the United States would use "massive retaliation" in response to even relatively minor Soviet encroachments on U.S. interests.

The shoe-pounding Soviet Premier Nikita Khrushchev countered with his own outrageous taunts. "We will bury you," he angrily proclaimed in 1960.

The harsh words of the spokesmen for the two countries were more than the background noise of the arms race: these messages were a key part of the psychological game of nuclear deterrence. Each side wanted its willingness to use force to be

16

taken seriously. Strident rhetoric was thought to be a way of demonstrating one's resolve.

Such fearsome declarations did more than reinforce the "credibility" of each side's deterrent. The tough talk fueled a tense rivalry in which the military establishments in both countries became obsessed with the need to develop more sophisticated and more destructive nuclear weaponry.

News of a technological advance by one side would give a sudden fright to the other, who would then immediately rush ahead to match—or best—the latest development. As the deadly competition expanded to encompass ever more complex weapons systems, the fear of "falling behind" grew into paranoia. Even a rumor or speculation about a possible "breakthrough" by one country could cause near-hysteria among the other side's military leaders.

This is not to say that there was not a real Soviet threat to the security of the United States. The Soviet military was steadily building weaponry that posed a mortal danger to this country. American leaders, however, seemed unable to assess the Soviet threat except in a habitually exaggerated way that confused real with imagined dangers.

Sometimes, of course, for obvious bureaucratic reasons, leaders in both the United States and U.S.S.R. found it useful to "cry wolf"—it was a way to get their military budgets increased. This political strategy was explained to President Truman in 1947 by Senator Arthur Vandenberg. In order to gain support for a military buildup, the senator noted, Truman would have to "scare hell out of the country." As the President roused the public against the "Red Menace," however, he lost considerable flexibility in dealing with the Soviet Union. He also set in motion a domestic political process that he could not control and which culminated in the excesses of the McCarthy period.

An example of the tendency to substitute inflammatory rhetoric for objective analysis was a landmark document prepared in 1950 during the deliberation over the H-bomb. The National Security Council report, NSC–68, was drafted under the direction of Paul Nitze (appointed thirty years later by President Reagan to negotiate with the Soviet Union on European nuclear weapons).

Many people found the report particularly disturbing. "What I read scared me so much that the next day I didn't go to the office at all," said Charles Murphy, one of Truman's top advisers. "I sat home and read this memorandum over and over, wondering what in the world to do about it."

One of the most alarming projections made by NSC–68 was that the Soviet Union would have 200 atomic bombs by 1954. Strategic analysts in the United States naturally began to wonder how the Soviets would deliver these bombs to America.

They had their answer when the Soviets displayed two new long-range bombers, the *Bear* and the *Bison,* in the 1954 and 1955 May Day parades in Moscow. Western observers counted the number of Soviet bombers as they flew overhead—information used by Air Force Intelligence to predict that the Soviets would have 600 to 700 bombers by 1959.

U.S. officials saw a looming military crisis, for the United States had no plans to produce anywhere near that number of bombers. Fearful of an imminent "bomber gap," the government stepped up production of its own intercontinental bomber, the B–52.

The bomber gap, in truth, existed only in the overactive imagination of U.S. Air Force officials eager to build up their own fleet of planes.

What Western embassy personnel in Moscow actually saw at the May Day parade, it was belatedly discovered, was not a huge squadron of new Soviet bombers; it was just the same handful of bombers circling over Moscow again and again. Flights in 1956 and 1957 by the U.S. photographic spy plane, the U–2, showed much lower production rates at Soviet airplane factories than the Air Force had forecast. The Air Force learned of its intelligence blunder but did not alter its plans for a large fleet of B–52s.

By 1961 there was indeed an imbalance in strategic bombers—the United States had over 600 long-range bombers and the Soviets only 190.

Still, the U.S. military establishment, as fearful as ever of falling behind—and as anxious as ever to enlarge its budget—was slow to acknowledge the lessons of the spurious bomber gap.

No sooner had that panic ceased when another nightmarish specter was presented to the nation by aroused military leaders: the United States, they announced, faced the terrifying prospect of being outgunned by long-range Soviet missiles. The "missile gap" became the catch phrase as they insisted on a U.S. program to counter this new threat.

The Soviets, like the United States, had indeed been working on long-range missiles. They successfully tested one in August 1957. Two months later, the Russians launched the world's first orbital satellite—*Sputnik.*

The United States panicked. The word *"Sputnik"* came to connote the prospect of a frightening Soviet technological superiority. Khrushchev compounded these fears with false claims that Soviet ICBMs could fly 6,000 miles and hit a "bull's-eye."

In November 1957, Air Force Intelligence warned that the Soviets could deploy 1,000 ICBMs by 1961. Other predictions were more ominous. "In three years, the Russians will prove to us that they have 3,000 ICBMs," Senator Stuart Symington claimed in March 1959. "Let that be on record."

The Eisenhower administration made the more moderate estimate that the Russians would have 300 missiles by the time the United States had 100. This revision did little to dispel fears that the Soviets were gaining the ability to wipe out U.S. nuclear forces in a massive sneak attack.

"At this point," warned *Life* magazine in March 1959, "we and our allies will be confronted with what the missilemen call missile blackmail . . . If we do not solve the missile problem, all other problems may become academic."

The Democratic candidate for President, John F. Kennedy, seized the issue during the 1960 presidential campaign. He placed the blame for this "missile problem" on the sluggish Eisenhower administration, which had failed to respond to the dire Soviet threat.

Once in office, Kennedy instructed Secretary of Defense

Robert McNamara to size up the situation. McNamara, relying on recently deployed spy satellites, promptly reported, in February 1961, that the Pentagon could find no evidence of extensive Soviet missile deployments. Later that year, the Defense Department estimated that the Soviets had a mere 50 ICBMs, in contrast to previous forecasts of 1,000 or more.

America, meanwhile, had not sat back idly. By the end of 1961, the United States had deployed nearly 200 Atlas ICBMs and had also accelerated production of the next generation of missiles—Titans and Minutemen. Once again, a "gap" in which the United States was reportedly behind turned out to be one in which it was really far ahead.

The U.S. missile buildup did not stop when we realized we were ahead though. The missile scare—according to Eisenhower science adviser Herbert York—spawned "a 1001 technical delights for remedying the situation. Most were expensive, most were complicated and baroque, and most were loaded more with engineering virtuosity than with good sense."

The Soviets, of course, felt compelled to respond to our initiatives, and their military had its own aggressive weapons-development program that added new and more sophisticated devices to its strategic arsenal. This, in turn, caused the Pentagon to look for more weapons to add to our arsenal. Like the bizarre "caucus race" Lewis Carroll invented in *Alice in Wonderland*—in which there were no rules to determine who had won—the United States and the Soviet Union competed against each other with no apparent goal in sight.

5

TO THE BRINK

"A missile is a missile. It makes no great difference whether you are killed by a missile from the Soviet Union or Cuba."
—Robert McNamara,
October 1962

THE RISKS inherent in an uncontrolled arms race were forcefully and unexpectedly demonstrated to the two superpowers when, on October 12, 1962, American U–2 reconnaissance planes photographed Soviet missile launching pads in Cuba.

In the United States, the fears and phobias of the preceding decade suddenly seemed to be confirmed: the Russian threat was materializing on our very doorstep.

But what were Russian missiles actually doing in Cuba? The Soviet government claimed that "the armaments and military equipment sent to Cuba" were "designed exclusively for defensive purposes." Despite protests from the Kennedy administration, there was a possible basis for this claim. The CIA had made numerous attempts to overthrow the Castro government, including the ill-fated 1961 invasion at the Bay of Pigs, which Kennedy had sanctioned. Castro might well have hoped the presence of Russian missiles would make the United States think twice before it tried again.

On the other hand, the Soviets in 1962 were far behind the

United States in ICBMs, and the stationing of missiles in Cuba may have been a reckless gamble on Khrushchev's part to compensate for U.S. superiority.

President Kennedy did not try to reach a negotiated agreement to have the missiles withdrawn. He rebuffed Khrushchev's suggestion of a summit meeting, until after the U.S. terms had been met. He also turned down Khrushchev's offer to exchange the missiles in Cuba for the U.S. Jupiter missiles located in Turkey, even though the obsolete Jupiters were already scheduled for retirement.

Instead, the President dramatically escalated the discovery of the Russian missiles into a full-scale crisis. In a televised broadcast on October 22, he announced that the United States could not tolerate the placement of "offensive" weapons near its shores. He also ordered a naval "quarantine" to prevent the shipment of weapons to Cuba.

One might ask how we could have objected so emphatically to the placement of missiles ninety miles from our shores while at the same time expecting the Russians to accept our missiles near the Soviet-Turkish border. Most officials in the Kennedy administration conceded privately, moreover, that the Cuban missiles did *not* pose a new threat to national security. "It is generally agreed that these missiles, even when fully operational, do not significantly alter the balance of power," wrote White House aide Theodore Sorensen in an October 17 memo.

Why, then, did the President take such a hard line?

Cold war psychology and domestic political factors were the main reasons. The nation may not have been imperiled, Roger Hilsman of the State Department explained, "but the Administration certainly was."

Throughout the cold war the American public had been told there could be no compromise with the forces of communism. "Nobody in the White House wanted to be soft," said a White House aide. "Everybody wanted to show they were just as daring and bold as everybody else."

Kennedy's course was also dictated by another domestic political consideration. The midterm elections were coming up in November, and a conciliatory stance might have led to a right-wing backlash.

"If you hadn't acted, you would have been impeached," Attorney General Robert Kennedy later told his brother.

Even former President Eisenhower speculated that "Kennedy might be playing politics with Cuba on the eve of Congressional elections."

More than politics was at stake. As Russian ships loaded with crated missiles approached the naval blockade, the administration reviewed its options. Plans under consideration ranged from a surgical strike on Cuban missile bases up to an all-out attack on Cuba. If pursued, these plans were likely to provoke Soviet countermoves.

The crisis was averted on October 26, when the United States, upon prompting from Robert Kennedy, decided to respond to a letter from Khrushchev. Subsequent negotiations led to a settlement in which the Soviets agreed to remove their missiles from Cuba and the United States promised never again to invade Cuba. The United States later removed its missiles from Turkey, maintaining the action had nothing to do with the Cuban affair.

The United States and the Soviet Union came harrowingly close to disaster during those two weeks in October. At one point President Kennedy rated the chances of nuclear war at 50-50. During the crisis, U.S. bombers circled the Soviet Union, prepared for attack. An American U–2 plane accidentally strayed off course, passing over Siberia while en route to Alaska. To make matters worse, U.S. bombers, sent to escort the U–2 home, met the plane over Soviet territory before heading back.

As the Soviet ships drew closer to Cuba on October 25, Robert Kennedy felt as if we "were on the edge of a precipice with no way off . . . President Kennedy had initiated the course of events, but he no longer had control over them."

6

A (VERY) LIMITED TEST BAN

"One of the political prices paid for getting wide accep-
tance of the Limited Test Ban Treaty in the Congress con-
sisted in a promise by the AEC to conduct an underground
test program vigorous enough to 'satisfy all our military
requirements'."

—*Herbert York, 1970*

THE CUBAN missile crisis forced both the United States and
the Soviet Union to recognize, at least temporarily, their mutual
interest in seeking ways to curb the nuclear arms race.

A growing international peace movement, moreover, was
also demanding action. Worldwide concern about the harmful
effects of fallout from atmospheric nuclear tests was a driving
force behind the "ban the bomb" protesters.

In July 1963, U.S. and Soviet representatives met in Moscow to negotiate a treaty limiting nuclear tests.

The testing of new nuclear warheads is a required step before any advanced weapon system can be deployed. Unless new
warheads are fully proof-tested, military planners would never
have adequate confidence in their reliability. They would not
want to deploy warheads simply on the basis of the designers'
unchecked predictions of how well they would work. Prohibit-

ing nuclear testing, therefore, would curtail major advances in weapons technology and greatly dampen the arms race.

Several years earlier, President Eisenhower had tried, unsuccessfully, to ban nuclear tests. The greatest opposition came not from the Russians but from the U.S. military.

"The real reason" for the American failure—British Prime Minister Harold Macmillan, a strong proponent of a comprehensive test ban, wrote in 1959—"is that the Atomic Commission and the Pentagon are very keen to go on *indefinitely* with experiments (large and small), so as to keep refining upon and perfecting the art of nuclear weapons."

A nonbinding moratorium on nuclear tests had been agreed upon by the United States, the Soviet Union, and Britain in 1958. One year later, President Eisenhower announced that America would no longer be bound by the agreement, but neither the United States, nor the other countries, resumed testing. The moratorium collapsed in September 1961 when the Soviets tested a nuclear bomb. The United States followed suit two weeks later.

In his bid for a test ban treaty in 1963, President Kennedy had to deal with congressional concerns that the Russians might somehow cheat and continue testing. To make sure the Soviets did not secretly conduct underground tests, the American proposal insisted on extensive on-site inspections.

"When I saw the details of what our experts would demand in the way of . . . inspection . . . the large area over which we would have helicopters range, and the number of holes we would have to drill, and that sort of thing," U.S. negotiator W. Averell Harriman said he became certain "they would never agree to it."

The Soviets had already made it clear they would agree to only a limited number of inspections and rejected the U.S. proposal. Further negotiations led to an agreement that banned atmospheric nuclear tests, but allowed for underground testing.

The treaty won Senate approval only after the administration agreed to a set of provisions promoted by Senator Henry Jackson and the Joint Chiefs of Staff. These conditions called for the United States to maintain readiness to resume atmospheric testing and, at the same time, pursue an "aggressive" underground testing program.

The Limited Test Ban Treaty was signed in July 1963 by the United States, the Soviet Union, and Great Britain. President Kennedy called the measure "an important first step."

In truth, the treaty was largely a cosmetic measure. It succeeded in reducing atmospheric fallout and the public relations problem arising from it, but it did little to impede the arms race. It merely pushed weapons testing underground. After the treaty was signed, both the United States and the Soviet Union proceeded to detonate far more nuclear devices than they had in the past.

"We learned that with a little ingenuity, you can do underground just about everything you can do in the air," an aide to Senator Jackson remarked.

With the arms race moving ahead in full swing, the treaty's only major effect, ironically, was to defuse the growing peace movement. For without the worrisome concern about fallout and the cancers and genetic defects it might cause, the public anxiety about weapons testing quickly abated. Some proponents of the treaty, such as George Kistiakowsky, Harvard chemist and science adviser to President Eisenhower, lamented years later that it ultimately did more to enhance the arms race than to control it.

President Kennedy himself, according to Jerome Wiesner, his science adviser, regretted that he had not asked for a stronger treaty. Traveling around the country in the summer of 1963 to help build support for the treaty, Kennedy said he found the public willing to accept more far-reaching arms control measures. He wished he had proposed them.

7

RULES OF THE GAME

"Rather than slowing the momentum of new weapons deployment, arms talks sometimes seem to encourage it. Why is this so?"

—*Richard Burt, 1978*

A FEW MONTHS after the Limited Test Ban Treaty was signed, President Kennedy was dead, his arms control ambitions buried with him. With the waning of the peace movement and the distraction of the Vietnam war, a low priority was assigned to curbing the nuclear arms race. President Johnson did propose a nuclear arms freeze in 1964, when the United States had a five to one lead in nuclear bombs. The Soviets rejected it, and the war made serious consideration of alternative arms control measures impossible.

As the number of Soviet missiles grew during the 1960s, Pentagon officials worried, as they had in the 1950s, that we were falling behind. They fretted over everything from Soviet civil defense efforts—a bomb-shelter gap—to the "mine-shaft gap." (This last fear apparently originated in the 1964 film *Dr. Strangelove.* The Soviet lead in mine shafts, it was argued by a character in the film, would enable them to save more citizens in a nuclear war than the United States. Eight years later, Defense Department officials were still discussing this absurdity before Congress.)

The U.S. military was particularly alarmed in the 1960s by the purported Soviet development of an antiballistic missile (ABM) defense system. Such a system, it was said, could use small, fast "antimissiles" to pluck U.S. warheads out of the air before they hit their intended targets in the Soviet Union. The U.S.S.R. could then hide behind a protective screen that made it invulnerable to a U.S. nuclear attack. Our nuclear deterrent would be neutralized, and they would no longer have anything to fear from us.

U.S. intelligence analysts repeatedly warned of growing Soviet ABM capabilities, which Khrushchev, with characteristic hyperbole, said could hit "a fly in outer space." An "ABM gap" was born. It proved to have no better foundation than the discredited—but, seemingly forgotten—scares about U.S. shortages of bombers and missiles.

One supposed Soviet "ABM system" built from 1964 to 1966, for example, later proved to be for defense against bombers, not ICBMs. The Soviets did subsequently attempt to build a real ABM around Moscow, but its ineffectiveness was soon apparent to both Soviet and U.S. military experts.

The Air Force, nonetheless, used the alleged ABM gap to justify a major increase in the number of U.S. nuclear bombs. Their goal was to acquire the capability to launch so many warheads that the U.S.S.R. would still be thoroughly devastated even if ABM defenses destroyed some of the incoming warheads.

To do this, the Pentagon decided to put several warheads on top of each U.S. missile. (In its terminology, the missiles would be equipped with MIRVs—multiple independently targetable re-entry vehicles.) An ICBM with one warhead can destroy only a single target, but a "MIRVed" ICBM can use its multiple warheads to destroy several targets which might be hundreds of miles apart. The Air Force liked the idea.

A further justification for switching to missiles with multiple warheads was the assertion that the Soviets would soon be able to do so. In 1965, U.S. intelligence predicted the Soviets could put multiple warheads on their ICBMs within five years. At the time there was no evidence that a Soviet MIRV program existed. The Air Force proceeded, nevertheless, with the development of multiple warheads, testing the first MIRVs in 1968 and deploying them by 1970.

Pentagon officials also used the Soviet ABM threat to promote the building of an ABM for the United States. In 1969, President Nixon urged Congress to support such a program. The congressional debate was highly charged. A major proponent of the ABM, Senator Richard Russell of Georgia, chairman of the Armed Services Committee, said, "If we have to start over again with another Adam and Eve, then I want them to be Americans and not Russians, and I want them on this continent and not in Europe."

The Senate approved the ABM proposal on a 50-50 vote, with Vice-President Agnew casting the tie-breaking ballot. Cold war rhetoric, rather than the merits of the issue, proved decisive. The testimony by leading scientists that such a system would probably not work, and would only encourage an expansion of the arms race, did not carry the day.

Having started to add multiple warheads to its missiles, thereby greatly augmenting its nuclear arsenal, President Nixon and his national security adviser Dr. Henry Kissinger decided, in 1969, that the United States was ready to sit down with the Soviets and talk about limiting the arms race.

After all, despite the alleged "gaps," we had at that point some 4,200 bombs in our strategic arsenal; the U.S.S.R. had only about 1,300. It was an advantageous time for the United States to try to slow down the arms race.

The U.S.-Soviet arms control negotiations, which began in Geneva in November 1969, became known as SALT—the "Strategic Arms Limitation Talks."

The representatives of both sides did not press for definitive arrangements that would end the arms race. Instead of such far-sighted statesmanship, they jockeyed to secure short-term advantages.

The Soviets weren't yet able to add multiple warheads to their missiles; the earlier U.S. estimates of their capability to do so had proved incorrect. U.S. negotiators were naturally willing to agree to an arms control treaty that simply limited the number of missiles. That would leave the Russians with their outdated single-warhead missiles while we took advantage of our MIRV technology. The Soviets, of course, wanted a treaty that banned multiple warheads.

As the discussions progressed, the United States was unwilling to budge on this issue. It was certainly easy for the Russians to "give up" MIRVs, which they didn't have, but why should America abandon such a large advantage as a monopoly on this new technology?

Of course, before the negotiations, proponents of MIRV had argued that its development would be a useful "bargaining chip"—an expendable weapon that could be bartered away for important Soviet concessions.

Once the talks were underway, however, the United States had already deployed MIRVS and decided they were too important to be traded away. The reluctance to part with one's supposed bargaining chips has occurred repeatedly in U.S.-Soviet arms negotiations. Today's bargaining chips routinely become permanent parts of tomorrow's nuclear arsenals.

(Defense Secretary Melvin Laird, for example, subsequently urged the development of cruise missiles—small, pilotless, low-flying aircraft that could be equipped with nuclear or conventional warheads—and said they could be given up in exchange for Soviet concessions at the next round of arms talks. By 1976 the Pentagon had declared the cruise missile off limits as a bargaining chip. "I didn't realize the Pentagon would fall in love with cruise missiles," Henry Kissinger confessed.)

In 1972, the two countries finally reached an agreement: the number of missile launchers each side could have was set, but not the number of warheads. The SALT treaty imposed a five-year freeze on offensive launchers, restricting the United States to 1,054 ICBMs and 656 submarine missiles and the Soviet Union to 1,400 ICBMs and 950 sub missiles. (Heavy bombers, a category in which the United States had a substantial edge, were not covered.)

Accompanying SALT was a treaty on defensive weapons under which the United States and the Soviet Union agreed to severely limit (and effectively ban) ABM systems. The meeting of the minds on this issue was not a sign that the two nations wanted to curb technological advances that were driving the arms race forward. It was merely an acknowledgment of what U.S. scientists had said during the 1969 debate on the subject: the ABM just wouldn't work satisfactorily to provide a defense against missile attacks.

The SALT agreement granted the Soviet Union a numerical advantage on launchers, but imposed no limit on warheads—the single most important indicator of strategic strength.

Kissinger, accordingly, considered the treaty a major coup for America. The United States, he told Congress, was interested in warheads, not launchers. "This was the theory behind SALT I, which froze numbers of at-that-time single warhead systems in the Soviet Union against multiple warhead systems in the U.S.," he explained.

Indeed, in the four years after SALT I went into effect, the United States added some 3,000 warheads to its nuclear arsenal, while the Soviets added about 600. The treaty clearly failed to halt the arms race.

The agreement was not, of course, intended to put a cap on arms development. Both sides regarded the measure as simply a way of *pacing* the arms race—setting a mutually agreed upon speed limit, the way such limits are posted on highways. Neither side wanted to cease their weapons buildup or to impose drastic curbs on its military establishment. Instead of setting a moderate limit on weapons deployment, akin to the 55 mph standard, they let future weapons acquisitions go forward full tilt. The arms race would remain very much a race.

In 1974, President Ford and Soviet Premier Brezhnev reached a further "arms control" agreement that showed how little interest either side had in actually constraining its military buildup. Under this agreement, reached during a meeting in

Vladivostock, each side would be "limited" to 2,400 strategic delivery vehicles—missiles and heavy bombers—of which 1,320 could be equipped with multiple warheads. The "ceilings" were so high that both nations could proceed rapidly with the expansion of their arsenals.

The irony in the "limits" adopted by the two countries was soon apparent. "Arms control negotiations are rapidly becoming the best excuse for escalating, rather than toning down the arms race," Herbert Scoville, Jr., former deputy director of the CIA, commented.

The nominal restrictions of the Vladivostock accord, moreover, would not stop the United States from making qualitative improvements in its weapons, such as increasing the accuracy of its nuclear warheads and refining MIRV technology. Nor would it keep the U.S.S.R. from the same pursuits.

The Soviets were thus free under the agreement to catch up with the United States, which is exactly what they tried to do. By 1975, they had developed, tested, and begun to deploy their own MIRV systems. This caused great fear in the U.S. military, which worried that with a large number of warheads, of increasing accuracy, the Soviets might acquire the capability to attack, and wipe out, U.S. ICBMs.

Before the days of MIRVed ICBMs, it would take at least one very accurate Soviet ICBM—more accurate than they had at the time—to destroy one U.S. ICBM, and vice versa. With the advent of MIRVs, though, a single ICBM carrying, say, ten warheads, could conceivably destroy ten ICBMs, giving the attacker a theoretical advantage. By providing a potential incentive for a preemptive first strike, the introduction of MIRVs has proved to be one of the most dangerous developments in the history of the arms race.

Had the United States not shortsightedly refused to ban MIRVs in the 1972 SALT Treaty, the Soviet countermove, to install the same threatening devices on their own ICBMs, might have been prevented.

"I wish I had thought through the implications of a MIRVed world," Henry Kissinger acknowledged in 1974.

8

THE EXTRAVAGANCE GAP

"If we don't spend enough on defense, nothing else will matter."

—*Richard Nixon,*
May 8, 1980

AS THE ARMS RACE continued during the 1970s—the SALT "limits" notwithstanding—the inevitable fright about "falling behind" once again gripped both U.S. and Soviet military authorities.

The United States had worked steadily for decades on the development of new weapons technology. The U.S.S.R., with its own substantial industrial and technological capability, had followed suit.

We usually had a technological edge—coming up with the first A-bombs, H-bombs, submarine-launched missiles, MIRVs, cruise missiles, and so forth—but the advantages we gained were never permanent. The Soviets always hurriedly struggled to match what we had achieved. It customarily took them about four or five years to catch up.

What happened when the Soviets tried to catch up?

The U.S. panicked. Like everything else about the arms race, fretting about the Soviet threat had become institutionalized. For years, a powerful military lobby in Washington had been supported by the recipients of the billions of dollars in Pentagon contracts. In the mid-1970s, new organizations such as the Committee on the Present Danger were formed, and they issued high-pitched demands for an all-out U.S. effort to build more weapons. Well-financed public-relations campaigns made frightening claims about menacing Soviet developments.

As in the 1950s and '60s, there were specious warnings about critical gaps in U.S. and Soviet forces. Like the nonexistent bomber and missile gaps, the new worries aroused substantial concern among Congress and the public. For example, there was said to be a "launcher gap." This was based on the claim that the Soviet Union had more strategic delivery vehicles (missiles and bombers) than the United States.

It was true, of course, that they had more launchers than the United States, just as they have more now. This does not convey any strategic military advantage, of course, because it is the number of deliverable warheads, a category in which the United States has always been ahead, that counts. As Henry Kissinger noted, it is warheads that kill people, not missile launchers.

A related gap, the "throw-weight gap," was cited as another cause for alarm. Soviet missiles, it was breathlessly pointed out, were generally much larger than ours and carried heavier bombs.

Only the naive observer would take this as an indication that we were "behind" the Soviets. Quite to the contrary. The United States could easily have built larger, heavier missiles, but we *chose* to build lighter, more sophisticated weaponry. Since the mid-1960s, the Defense Department has concentrated on deploying large numbers of smaller nuclear bombs that do more damage than big bombs with the same net explosive power.

The main reason the Soviets have such large missiles, which use liquid propellant as fuel, is that their backward chemical industry has been slow to produce the type of solid propellant fuel the United States uses in its more compact missiles. The difference in the size of U.S. and Soviet missiles is a sign of *their* weakness, not ours.

The major scare story of the 1970s—the most celebrated gap of all—focused on the CIA "discovery," in 1976, that Soviet military expenditures were twice as large as the agency had believed. A new strategic imbalance materialized practically overnight: the spending gap.

According to Richard Pipes, Paul Nitze, and other members of a 1976 special review group appointed by CIA Director George Bush, the Soviets were devoting 11 to 13 percent of their GNP to defense, not the 6 to 8 percent the CIA had previously estimated. The United States expended only about 6 percent of its GNP on defense and was therefore said to be dangerously behind in the arms race, because it was being "outspent" by the Russians.

The mutilated logic of such a claim ought to be immediately apparent: it is not an enemy's spending level that kills you, it's his weapons. On the battlefield it doesn't make any earthly difference whether the enemy has spent a dollar or a hundred dollars per bullet. What counts is not the budget for bullets but the number he's got on the battlefield, his marksmens' courage and skill, and so forth. What it cost to produce the bullets and rifles indicates how well the enemy's economy performs; his military capability is a separate subject.

The CIA figures, accordingly, did not reveal any new Soviet *military* advantage or disadvantage; if they showed anything at all, it was that the Soviets had an inefficient economy in which it cost an exorbitant amount to manufacture military hardware. We should have been pleased to discover that their defense industry was so inept; instead we were alarmed.

The reason for this reaction was, in large part, attributable to the efforts of the Committee on the Present Danger. Formed in 1976 by Paul Nitze and others who wished to lobby for a larger defense budget, the group issued strident pronouncements about the growing Soviet threat and urged an American counterbuildup. The Soviet strategic arms buildup was "without precedent in history," it declared, and was "reminiscent of Nazi Germany's rearmament in the 30s."

In 1978, the committee announced that the United States

had cut military expenditures by two-thirds, while the Soviets had doubled their defense spending. "I don't think it's fair to say that it's a race when only one side has been racing," their report, entitled "Peace with Freedom," proclaimed.

Nitze, in fact, was using the same arguments he had submitted to President Truman in 1950, when he supervised the preparation of National Security Council document 68. He argued then that the Soviets were spending 20 percent of their GNP on defense and that the United States should do likewise.

Nitze, evidently, had not learned, in the intervening quarter of a century, the folly of basing military planning on the GNP.

What, after all, is the GNP? It is an accounting concept: a convenient figure that indicates the overall level of economic activity in a country in a given year, its "gross national product." It sums up the total value of all the goods and services delivered to consumers (for example, houses that were built, cars sold) as well as a country's other major economic achievements, such as the value of new equipment produced.

The GNP can be related to defense spending, of course, in the sense that it indicates how much productive capacity the country has and how much it might be able to spend on defense. But GNP does not determine what the *required* levels of defense spending ought to be. That depends on the kinds of military threats that exist, on what needs to be done about them, and on what this costs to achieve. It hardly makes any sense, therefore, to fix defense spending as a percent of GNP, which means to keep increasing it as the GNP grows.

The GNP, after all, increases every time someone purchases new clothing or a brewery buys a new piece of equipment. Surely, the production of strategic warheads does not have to increase every time the trends in fashion send people out for new wardrobes or the thirst for beer dictates bigger breweries.

Faulty logic aside, the claim that the United States had meekly refrained from building its military forces was utterly incorrect. The United States spent over $1 trillion on defense in the 1970s and was then spending more than at any period in its history except for World War II and the height of the Korean and Vietnam wars.

The further claim that the Soviets were spending 50 percent more on defense than the United States resulted from bogus bookkeeping by the CIA. The agency's "creative accounting" of Soviet expenditures was based on the assumption that Soviet military manpower was paid according to standard U.S. military allowances. In other words, to compute Soviet spending on military personnel, the CIA multiplied the number of Soviet soldiers by *U.S. Army* pay scales.

The error, of course, is that Soviet armed forces are mainly composed of conscripts who receive only about one-fifth as much as the average U.S. soldier. "By computing Soviet manpower costs at American rates, one discovers a large Soviet defense manpower budget of over $50 billion that exists only in American documents," Congressman Les Aspin, a former Pentagon official, observed.

Also, since the CIA estimates of Soviet expenditures were based on U.S. pay scales, every time *our* soldiers got a raise, the CIA's accounts showed a rise in Russian defense spending.

The accounting was defective for many other reasons, such as the CIA's neglect of the fact that U.S. defense activities are closely tied to those of our European allies—allies far wealthier than the Eastern European countries allied to the U.S.S.R. by the Warsaw Pact. Combined, the United States and its partners in NATO outspent the Soviet Union and Warsaw Pact by several hundred billion dollars in the 1970s and continue to outspend them today.

When all these factors are taken into account, the spending picture looks considerably different. "It is time that the American public understands that these quotes about being outspent by the USSR are just plain inaccurate," Senator William Proxmire, chairman of the Joint Economic Committee, stated. "They are nonsense, balderdash, phony, fake, and I might add, untrue."

9

THE MYTH OF VULNERABILITY

"The Soviets don't have to pull the trigger. They have superiority. They've got a deterrent and we don't, and that's the window of vulnerability."

—*Richard DeLauer,*
1982

NO MATTER how much it spends on arms, the U.S. military never seems to be able to buy peace of mind. The latest multi-billion-dollar Pentagon program is barely paid for when demands for even larger expenditures are pressed on Congress and the administration in office.

The most awesome danger to our security, the Pentagon began to argue in the late seventies, arose from the Soviet's newfound ability—as a result of MIRVed ICBMs—to "wipe out" U.S. Minuteman missiles in a surprise "first strike." With U.S. land-based missiles reduced to "sitting ducks," there for the taking, officials feared that the country could not adequately deter Soviet aggression.

According to the Joint Chiefs of Staff, the vulnerability of U.S. missiles would probably "affect the Soviet perception of the military balance in such a way that it will embolden them to act with less restraint in international affairs." As a result of their superiority, the Soviets don't have to attack or even threaten

38

to attack, the official reasoning continued. Our unilateral restraint, based on our knowledge of what would transpire in the event of war, it was said, would be enough to tip the balance of power in their favor.

"The real risk is not so much nuclear war as nuclear blackmail," explained Eugene Rostow, former head of the Committee on the Present Danger. Committee member Paul Nitze has worried about this problem since 1956, when he compared the situation to "a game of chess. The atomic queens may never be brought into play; they may never actually take one of the opponent's pieces. But the position of the atomic queens may still have a decisive bearing on which side can safely advance a limited-war bishop or even a cold-war pawn."

There was no tangible U.S. military weakness to justify the anxious talk about a "window of vulnerability." We are dealing, instead, with another manifestation of cold war paranoia. For surely it is nonsense to conclude that the Soviets would ever be tempted to launch a bolt-out-of-the blue attack on U.S. ICBMs. This is so even if the Soviets *could* knock out all of these missiles. (We will take up this technical issue separately.)

To appreciate the U.S.S.R.'s reluctance to start a nuclear war one does not have to make any controversial assumptions about Soviet morality and good will. However blackhearted the United States may presume this adversary to be, the Soviets still have to consider that following their first strike they would face a U.S. "second-strike": a punishing retaliatory blow.

Even if a Soviet first strike destroyed every last ICBM in the U.S. stockpile—all 1,052 Minuteman and Titan missiles based in the Great Plains—the United States would still be left with the bulk of its nuclear firepower intact aboard bombers and submarines. All told, the 100 U.S. bombers kept on alert and the more than twenty submarines on patrol at all times could respond to a first strike by dropping more than 4,000 hydrogen bombs on the Soviet Union. These bombs could destroy every major Soviet city 20 times over. Just a single Poseidon sub, it will be recalled, could destroy every major city in the Soviet Union. Surely no Soviet planner, however strong his ill will toward us, would wish to attack the United States at such a cost as the obliteration of his homeland.

The think-tank analysts who invent "scenarios" for theoretical Soviet first strikes work out their calculations in an antiseptic, computerized dream world. The players—sitting in air-conditioned rooms as they engage in "war games" where no real blood is shed—are free to take suicidal risks. This is hardly a model of real decision-making.

"I have always found the hypothetical nuclear scenarios inherently implausible," Lieutenant General Kelley Burke, chief of Air Force research and development, acknowledges. "I've never seen one that I thought likely to transpire."

Threatened by the risk of a massive second strike, it is difficult to believe that Soviet planners, in cold blood, would ever attempt what former Defense Secretary Harold Brown called the "cosmic roll of the dice."

There are technical reasons, moreover, that the "window of vulnerability" can be regarded as just another cold war mastermyth spun together out of a fearful misunderstanding of the true situation facing the United States.

A successful Soviet first strike against U.S. ICBMs requires pinpoint accuracy, as well as a high degree of reliability in missile launch and in weapons detonation. Our missiles are housed underground in "hardened" concrete silos designed to withstand nearby thermonuclear blasts. They can be destroyed only if they receive what are essentially direct hits. There are more than a thousand silos, and a thousand Soviet bull's-eyes would be required to knock them all out.

This would be quite a feat, for nuclear warheads, once launched toward their destinations by powerful rockets, are in free flight, like the bullets fired from a gun. Although minor corrections are possible, their course cannot be altered like that of piloted weapons. To knock out U.S. missiles, moreover, Soviet warheads have to travel thousands of miles, over trajectories never before tested, and land within a few hundred feet of their targets. To raise the chances of knocking out U.S.

missiles, several Soviet warheads would have to be aimed at each missile, timed in such a way so that the explosion of one warhead would not accidentally destroy the other warheads intended for the same target. (The problem of interference between warheads intended for the same target has been dubbed "fratricide.")

Can it be done?

"It's something we will never be able to practice so you'll never know," said Admiral Powell Carter, the Navy's Director of Strategic and Theater Nuclear Warfare. "We do our very best to find out. But we'll never be sure and the Soviets will never be sure."

One problem is accuracy. Neither U.S. nor Soviet ICBMs have ever been fired over the North Pole, which is the direction they would have to travel in a strategic exchange. Even slight deviations from estimated gravitational forces and atmospheric conditions could send them off course. Short of substantial testing, many scientists consider this problem of missile "bias" to be technically insurmountable.

Neither we nor the Soviets know precisely how accurate their missiles are. If anything, we tend to overestimate Soviet missile accuracy in the same way we overstate their general military capabilities. According to Jim Miller, head of the ballistic missile branch at the Defense Intelligence Agency, Soviet SS–17 ICBMs "do not have an acceptable PK [probability-of-kill] capability." They do not, that is, have a very high probability of landing close enough to the intended target. Referring to the SS–18s that the United States is especially worried about, he said, "The guy who designed the [Mod–2] post-boost vehicle is probably in Siberia because everything that you could do wrong in the design of a post-boost vehicle, he did. He really goofed it." The Mod–4, the latest delivery vehicle for the SS–18s has "the best accuracy of all their fourth generation systems," but "that is still not good enough," Miller believes.

Reliability poses another major uncertainty for the aggressor. Just as there have been problems in the space program with the launching of rockets, the military is bound to have comparable problems in launching ballistic missiles. The Soviets can't know in advance how many of their missiles will fail during launch or at some point in the boost stage, or how many warheads will fail to detonate.

The Soviets would also run the risk that U.S. ICBMs had been placed on "launch under attack," meaning that they would be launched *before* they were destroyed. The U.S., that is, based on data from its satellite and radar early warning systems, might decide to fire its ICBMs as soon as it detected signals of incoming Soviet missiles. The Soviet warheads would then strike empty missile silos.

Considering all the various technical difficulties, there would be little basis for confidence in the minds of Soviet planners that a first strike would be anything other than an insanely risky venture.

"Nothing has been put forward which technologically supports the belief that we (or the Soviets) could, with any degree of confidence, expect to hit one silo at ICBM range, let alone 1,000 of them distributed over an area equal to one-third of the United States," an editorial in *Strategic Review* noted in 1981.

At a minimum, some fraction of the U.S. ICBMs would escape destruction, and there would be the risk that all of them could be launched first, before the Soviet warheads came close to them. These risks are compounded by the further dissuading factor—the second-strike capability of U.S. bombers and submarines.

Such are the factors that would weigh on the mind of the would-be aggressor. There is no vulnerability in U.S. strategic forces, accordingly, that would conceivably tempt the Soviet Union to attack. "They would deter anyone who is not crazy" former Secretary of Defense Harold Brown observes.

As far as ICBM "vulnerability" is concerned, "there is really no reason why one has to do anything," Richard Garwin, physicist and leading Defense Department technical adviser, has concluded.

His clients, however, disagreed. Insisting on the need to respond to the Soviet threat to our ICBMs, the Air Force went ahead with plans for building a new supermissile, the MX.

According to a plan announced by President Jimmy Carter in 1979, 200 MX missiles would be deployed in an immense new missile complex stretching across Utah and Nevada (and possibly farther). In a nuclear shell game, the United States would play hide-and-seek with the Russians, shuttling missiles back and forth along "racetracks" among 4,600 concrete storage bunkers. Unlike the Minuteman ICBMs, "sitting ducks" in their stationary silos, the mobile MX would supposedly be invulnerable to attack from the Soviets, who would never know where the missiles were. Cost estimates for the new missile system went as high as $100 billion.

Of course, if the Soviets could make pinpoint attacks on Minuteman silos, they could presumably also destroy MX storage bunkers. They would not have to know exactly which of them housed the missiles. They could just bomb all 4,600 bunkers.

The flaws in the Air Force plan for the MX prompted Garwin to observe, "We've done stupid things before, but never on this scale."

10

THE IMPOTENCE COMPLEX

"It is time to wake up the sleeping giant ... We must restore our military strength—and our castrated CIA, by the way."

—*Richard Nixon,*
1980

RIDICULE of the MX did not dampen official enthusiasm for the new supermissile. The Pentagon still insisted that the expensive program was urgently needed to cure America's strategic inferiority.

The supposed disease, however, was purely psychosomatic: there was no weakness in our nuclear deterrent that demanded such a quack remedy.

As the balance sheet of U.S. and Soviet nuclear forces amply demonstrates, the nuclear might on each side is essentially equivalent, not dangerously imbalanced. By any reasonable standard, the United States and the U.S.S.R. are overmuscled nuclear giants.

The truth, though, was that the United States, by the late 1970s, didn't *feel* like one anymore.

What was the underlying problem? It wasn't just another round of cold war paranoia that had spread throughout the

44

nation. It was much more than that. America, by the late seventies, to borrow the buzz word from a popular advertisement, had come down with a bad case of the "blahs."

Vietnam, Watergate, the energy crisis, inflation, unemployment, Iran, and Afghanistan: the list of setbacks was a long one. These were more than just isolated difficulties. They added up to a decade of nonstop trauma that deeply affected the national mood.

No longer was there the ebullience of the fifties—when the country, number one in economic, technological, and military prowess, felt secure in its position as leader of the "Free World." The great economic engine that produced the marvel of ever-expanding material gain was sputtering and backfiring. No longer did the country look forward with confidence to a future of limitless affluence.

Everything had changed. The country had embarrassed itself with blunders ranging from the war in Southeast Asia to the accident at Three Mile Island. It had been bullied by the O.P.E.C. oil cartel and threatened by Japanese competition. And it had been humiliated by ABSCAM, by the ineffectual leaders voted into office, and by the dearth of ideas for tackling the economic and social problems it faced.

"What do you expect?" the owner of a household appliance store in Brooklyn said after U.S. helicopters broke down during the rescue mission in Iran. "The U.S. can't even produce a good toaster anymore. Now nothing works."

It was inevitable that America's self-doubt would lead to worries about its nuclear deterrent. After all, at the heart of deterrence has been a psychological strategy: to instill enough fear in the Soviets that they would be reluctant to attack us. But how could we expect the Russians to fear us if we, ourselves, *felt* so weak and inadequate?

Moreover, U.S. military leaders had talked so much about the vulnerability of our missiles that we had lost a psychological edge to the Russians, even if the missiles were not really vulnerable. "To a certain extent, we have shot ourselves in the foot," Pentagon official William Perry conceded. "We have inflicted these problems on ourselves by the way we have advertised them."

The popular view thus arose—greatly encouraged by the vigorous public relations campaign of military lobby groups, the Moral Majority, and the New Right—that the United States was a 98-pound weakling confronting the massive Russian bear.

"The Russians could walk right in and take over without firing a shot," said fundamentalist preacher Jerry Falwell. "They could do that any time between now and the mid-1980s—and long after that if we continue with the Carter Administration's nondefense policy." When asked how the Russians could walk in, Falwell replied, "Across the Mexican border."

Worry about U.S. inferiority led the Committee on the Present Danger and other lobby groups to oppose U.S. efforts to extend the SALT Treaty with the U.S.S.R. Since 1972, negotiations on a SALT II Treaty had been underway. When they culminated in 1979, there was a tentative agreement, very much in the interest of the United States, under which the Soviet Union would have had to eliminate about 10 percent of its ICBM force, cutting into the portion of its nuclear arsenal that we were most worried about. However advantageous the SALT II Treaty may have been for this country, it was attacked as a measure that would preserve the Soviet Union's alleged superiority. After the U.S.S.R. invaded Afghanistan in December 1979, President Carter withdrew the treaty from the Senate and it became an issue in the 1980 presidential elections.

Ronald Reagan, an opponent of the treaty, was swept into office after a campaign that promoted an assertive new defense policy. He promised the American people a program to restore the country to greatness.

"It is time for us to start a [military] buildup," he urged, "and it is time for us to build to the point that no other nation on this earth will ever dare raise a hand against us, and in this way we will preserve world peace."

PART II

THE NEW
BUILDUP

11

MORE OF EVERYTHING

"We never articulated our defense strategy in a coherent way. [There is the perception] that we're just sinking bucks into defense without an overall strategy."
                    Secretary of State Alexander Haig, 1982

THE CURRENT U.S. military buildup is based on a simple principle that was stated by Hans Mark, the outgoing Secretary of the Air Force under President Carter: "We need everything, as soon as possible," he told an interviewer.

In February 1981, with the new administration in office only a few weeks, the Pentagon was ready with an across-the-board plan for increased spending. The plan included a long list of proposals that military leaders had been promoting for several years. The President adopted the Pentagon's plan and asked Congress to authorize the most expensive arms program in peacetime history.

The defense package endorsed by President Reagan called for more than $1.6 trillion to be spent over a five-year period, during which the military budget would more than double. Deep cuts in spending for nonmilitary programs were proposed to permit this massive allocation of federal monies to the Pentagon.

The Department of Defense, according to the White House budget director David Stockman, "got a blank check" from the

49

new administration. Military leaders were still not satisfied. The top officers of all four military services contend that the amount slated for the five-year program will be insufficient. Senior officials estimate that an additional $750 billion may be required to close the gap with the U.S.S.R.

The administration plan covered everything from taking old battleships out of mothballs to promoting the development of Star Wars technologies for fighting nuclear wars in space. At its center stood a $180 billion strategic "modernization" program that President Reagan said "will signal our resolve to maintain the strategic balance."

Among other things, the buildup means adding 50 to 100 MX missiles, 100 B–1 bombers, 12 Trident submarines, thousands of cruise missiles, and 17,000 additional nuclear warheads to the U.S. arsenal by the end of the decade. It includes continued development of the new Stealth bomber designed to elude Soviet air defense and production of the neutron bomb. New tanks, helicopters, surveillance planes, tactical aircraft, battleships, aircraft carriers, and chemical weapons are also planned. The rejection of any element of this program, President Reagan said, "would be a dangerous and misleading signal of weakening American resolve in the face of an ever growing Soviet challenge."

Congress approved the Reagan plan with only slight modifications and without detailed study. The plan deserves careful analysis, however, for, if left unchanged, it will be the basis for a new, open-ended, and even more dangerous arms race with the U.S.S.R. Three parts of the plan—the MX missile, the B–1 bomber, and the proposals for an expanded "new" Navy—merit particular attention.

THE MX MISSILE

The MX missile is a cornerstone of the administration's program to close the so-called window of vulnerability. Bigger, more accurate, and more deadly than current U.S. Minuteman missiles, MX is the number-one symbol of America's determination to attain "strategic superiority."

The Carter racetrack plan for deploying the MX had met with strong political opposition in Utah and Nevada. The Reagan administration scrapped that "basing mode." Still, it could not readily decide where it *would* put the new missiles.

A Pentagon advisory panel on the MX, headed by Nobel Prize-winning physicist Charles Townes, was established by Defense Secretary Caspar Weinberger to recommend new basing modes for the missile. The idea that most impressed Secretary Weinberger was the Big Bird proposal, which involved launching the missiles from a special new aircraft. The planes would be powered by highly efficient engines and could remain aloft for several days without refueling. They are not available now, but their development is a possibility that might be studied further, the panel concluded.

The administration then decided it would "temporarily" install the MX missiles in existing Titan silos while it searched for a permanent basing mode. The Pentagon changed its mind again, and selected existing Minutemen silos. Both proposed solutions caused immediate embarrassment to the Pentagon, for they obviously left unchanged the problem they were intended to solve: the supposed vulnerability of missiles, in fixed sites, that were "sitting ducks" for the Russians to shoot at.

In December 1981, by a vote of 90 to 4, the Senate rejected the "interim" plan to place the MX in existing silos. It made no sense, the members decided, to build a missile without knowing what to do with it.

The search for an invulerable basing mode has continued. An old idea recently resurrected by the Pentagon has been to place the missiles so far underground that the Soviets couldn't possibly destroy them. (A version of this plan was mentioned in the 1964 film *Dr. Strangelove*. "I think we ought to look at this from the military point of view," General Buck Turgidson advised. "Supposing the Russians stashed away some big bombs, and we didn't. When they came out in 100 years, they could take over.")

The Air Force, however, has rejected proposals for deep underground missile basing (sometimes referred to by its acronym DUMB) at least nine times in the past 20 years, primarily because it would cost too much. There are also serious doubts as to whether it would be possible to burrow through tons of rubble from surface missile bursts and actually launch the buried missiles after a nuclear attack.

The MX basing mode currently favored by the Pentagon is called "Dense Pack." Under this arrangement, MX missiles would be clustered close together and defended with a ballistic missile defense system, something which has not yet been invented. Critics of the plan have called it "Dunce Pack." A significant defect is that the Soviets might deploy huge blockbuster warheads that could knock out several of the closely spaced missiles in a single blow. The deployment of ballistic missile defenses would also require the abrogation of the 1972 ABM Treaty. Although of dubious reliability, these systems would probably spur the Soviets to develop missile defenses of their own, leading to a costly and dangerous new stage in arms competition.

"This whole MX thing borders on the silly," Senator Mark Andrews, a conservative Republican from North Dakota, observed. "We're building a Rolls Royce and we don't have a garage to put it in . . . I hope we can find a home for this waif before we make too many of them."

THE B–1 BOMBER

The B–1 bomber, a long-standing Air Force priority previously rejected by Congress and the Carter administration, was revived as part of the Reagan defense package. Despite serious reservations, Congress voted funds for the proposal.

Like the MX, the B–1 is a symbol to demonstrate America's "will" to enhance its strategic strength by replacing its "aging" B–52s. The B–1 is expensive, even for a political symbol: the entire fleet of 100 bombers is estimated to cost $20 to 40 billion.

Chief among the doubts over the B–1, which critics call the "$40 billion flying Edsel," is that it is likely to become obsolete before it is deployed. President Reagan has replied that the "fact that its one mission of penetrating enemy airspace might be eliminated in a few years time does not mean you scrap it. There will be other purposes for which it can be used, so it isn't a total loss." The President has not yet identified what those "other purposes" might be, and many members of Congress remain skeptical.

In response to the critics, Defense Secretary Weinberger modified his initial statement that the plane could penetrate Soviet air defenses "until 1990." His revised estimate was that it could do so "until well into the 1990's." More recently, he extended the capability "well into the next century." He has not explained how this has suddenly become possible.

The best way to evade Soviet radar is to fly an aircraft that presents a small radar target and keep it as close to the ground as possible. This is best achieved with a small, light aircraft. But the proposed B–1 will be only 2 percent lighter than the B–52, which the Air Force considers too heavy for future strategic missions.

Even if the B–1 had a slight edge over B–52s in eluding Soviet air defenses, it would still not be as effective as B–52s armed with the $11 billion worth of cruise missiles that the Pentagon has recently ordered. These are "stand-off" weapons: tiny, low-flying missiles which can be launched 1,000 miles from the Soviet border, so that strategic bombers won't have to fly over the Soviet Union in order to destroy targets.

The days of long-range penetrating bombers are numbered; bombers in the future will be shuttle devices that bring cruise missiles within range. "Does the U.S. need to buy a tremendous penetration capability if all that is needed is a stand-off platform?" asks former Army intelligence officer Michael Johnson. "Must the new aircraft do much more than fly?"

THE "NEW" NAVY

Of all the services, the Navy has perhaps the most ambitious goal: expanding its fleet from 450 to 600 ships by the end of the decade. The effort to regain U.S. "naval superiority" has been undertaken with little explanation as to what will be done in the missile age with all of the old-fashioned surface ships acquired.

The administration suggests that it plans to challenge the Soviet fleet wherever there is a sea.

Admiral Hyman Rickover, the recently retired head of the U.S. nuclear submarine program, thinks it is "nonsense" to try to match the Soviets ship for ship. "Take the number of nuclear subs," he told Congress. "I'll hit right close to home. I see no reason why we have to have just as many as the Russians do. At a certain point you get [to] where it's sufficient. What's the difference whether we have 100 nuclear subs or 200? . . . You can sink everything on the oceans several times over with the number we have, and so can they."

A conspicuous entry in the current Navy budget is $7 billion earmarked for the construction of two nuclear aircraft carriers. "If you know anything about nuclear aircraft carriers," Wall Street analyst Gary Reich explains, "you understand that construction costs are just the basic expense. It's like building a car without all the extras. After you build the aircraft carrier . . . you've got to spend just about an equal amount putting airplanes, guns and other gear on it."

The major problem with large aircraft carriers is that they provide an immensely vulnerable target for enemy missiles, bombs, or torpedoes. Only a few Harpoon antiship missiles, at a cost of $700,000 apiece, are needed to destroy a $3.5 billion carrier. According to Admiral Rickover, a carrier would last "about two days" in an all-out war with the Soviet Union. Such vessels have largely outlived their usefulness in the face of today's advanced weapons technology.

Another controversial item on the Navy's agenda is the proposal to spend $1.5 to $3.5 billion to renovate four mammoth battleships. Proponents of the idea, such as Senator John Warner of the Armed Services Committee, the former Secretary of the Navy, argue that the ships have "tremendous symbolic value that harkens back to the days of gunboat diplomacy."

What can be done with such symbols, in the missile age,

remains the question. During the war in the Falklands, a single radar-guided Argentine missile (costing $200,000) destroyed the British warship *Sheffield,* which cost $50 million. Two electronically-guided British torpedoes sunk Argentina's largest naval vessel, the *General Belgrano.*

The Pentagon has not yet devised a way to "modernize" antiquated surface ships in order to thwart the modern technology that can be used to destroy them.

The current U.S. defense "program," as the three foregoing examples illustrate, reduces to a grab bag of spending proposals.

"To paraphrase Will Rogers, I think this Administration has never seen a weapons system that it doesn't like," Congressman Les Aspin, a former Pentagon official, commented.

In its haste to draw up a budget, the Reagan administration failed to sort out priorities. "They didn't go into the process with any conceptual framework," former Pentagon official Phillip Odeen commented. "They just said to the services: 'What do you want?'" The resultant budget amounted to little more than a compilation of military "wish lists."

12

FIRST STRIKE

"We in the military don't go into these organizations and spend our lives at it to try to fight a war to a draw. Our business is to fight a war to victory. So we're constantly trying to get better, more accurate, more powerful weapons . . ."

—*Rear Admiral Gene LaRocque, 1981*

ASSOCIATED with the current nuclear weapons buildup is an emerging new strategy on how such devices are to be used. At its core, the current policy ratifies a dangerous change in U.S. nuclear strategy that has been evolving for several years: the shift from a defensive posture, in which an assured retaliatory capability is the main goal, to a new, aggressive stance in which the United States would develop the means to fight, and "win," a nuclear war.

Many U.S. military leaders have never liked the prevailing stalemate in which the only "use" for nuclear weapons is to hold the other side at bay. Standard military doctrine is based on fighting to victory, not sitting passively for years in a nervous standoff with the enemy. Hence the desire to move beyond assured retaliation to a first-strike capability.

Although nuclear war has often been called "unthinkable,"

both the United States and the Soviet Union have cadres of experts who do nothing but think about it. Each side looks for the edge in technology or some clever stratagem that would allow it to best the other in a nuclear confrontation.

If war had broken out between the superpowers in 1954, for example, recently declassified documents state that the United States had a plan to launch a massive strike that would have left the Soviet Union a "smoking radiation ruin at the end of two hours."

General Curtis LeMay, then commander of the Strategic Air Command, stated "that if the U.S. is pushed in the corner far enough, we would not hesitate to strike first."

Another recently declassified document, a memorandum from Secretary of Defense Robert McNamara to President Kennedy written in November 1962, stated: "It has become clear to me the Air Force proposals are based on the objective of achieving a first-strike capability." McNamara emphatically rejected such a goal, concluding it was unattainable, but proponents within the Pentagon never abandoned it.

The general desire for a first-strike capability, and having the means to accomplish it, are, of course, two different things. What has happened in recent years, however, is that new technology has come along that has made preemptive strikes more feasible, at least in theory. The main development has been the improved accuracy of nuclear warheads.

Accuracy did not matter that much in the days of the first ICBMs. With a deterrent posture based on the threat of destroying the other side's cities, the targets were big and easy to hit. Since the missiles carried such large blockbusters, it did not make a great difference where exactly the bombs exploded over a given city. The entire metropolis would still be destroyed.

Pinpoint accuracy is needed in a first strike against an opponent's missiles, however. The attacker has to score almost dead hits on small, well-protected targets: the opponent's hardened ICBM silos. The goal of such a strike would be to knock out the other side's forces, leaving them unable to respond to an attack. Thus, each jump in missile accuracy has brought the

United States and the U.S.S.R. closer and closer to a theoretical first-strike capability against the other's ICBMs.

These technological developments were cited during the late 1970s by U.S. military leaders lobbying for a change in strategic policy. They wanted the United States to abandon the notion of "mutual assured destruction," under which the two sides supposedly held each other in check by the threat of wiping out their respective civilian populations. Instead, they wanted to target our warheads principally on Soviet ICBMs and other military installations.

In July 1979, by means of Presidential Directive 59, President Carter approved the "counterforce" targeting plan that the Pentagon had been developing over the years.

The present administration, greatly extending the plan, wants a full-scale U.S. nuclear war-fighting capability. It calls for the development of forces able to "render ineffective the total Soviet (and Soviet allied) military and political power structure." This would include the ability to make lightning strikes against the U.S.S.R. that would "decapitate" the Soviet leadership and its command and control system, thereby hindering retaliation against us. Under this plan, the United States would acquire the means to fight a protracted nuclear war. The goal would be to have strategic forces that can "prevail and be able to force the Soviet Union to seek earliest terminations of hostilities on terms favorable to the U.S." The United States, in short, wants the ability to win an all-out nuclear war should one break out.

A key weapon in the new offensive strategy is the MX missile, which would be able to deliver its ten warheads—each the equivalent of 30 Hiroshimas—to widely separated targets in the U.S.S.R. The planned MX would be twice as accurate and more than three times as powerful as the most advanced Minuteman missiles. The new missile, according to General B. L. Davis of the Strategic Air Command, "will convince the Soviets that the sanctuary that has thus far been accorded his ICBM silos can no longer be assured."

The MX is unabashedly a first-strike weapon. Such a

superaccurate weapon is obviously not needed for a retaliatory attack on Soviet cities. There is little point, moreover, in having a weapon capable of destroying the enemy's ICBM silos unless you intend to use it first. After all, the silos would presumably be empty if the other side had started the war.

"It has proved difficult for us to eliminate a first-strike capability from MX," General Lewis Allen, the former Air Force chief of staff, admitted.

The Trident II submarine currently under development will also give the United States "preemptive capability," according to Pentagon scientist Richard DeLauer. A single sub will carry 24 missiles, each armed with 10 to 14 warheads, that can unleash the equivalent of six Hiroshimas on 240, or more, Soviet targets. With precise position information provided by satellite, these missiles will be accurate enough to threaten Soviet ICBM silos. Because they can be launched close to the Soviet Union, they are potentially much faster than the MX, allowing the Soviets as little as ten minutes' warning time.

A first-strike capability, while appealing in terms of traditional military thinking, would buy more danger than security for the United States, even if it were technically feasible.

It would mean, for example, that in a crisis, the Soviets would face what is termed a "launch or lose" situation: if they hesitated, their weapons might be destroyed before they could fire a shot. Thus, instead of being deterred by our menacing capability, they might be tempted to lash out at us while they still had the chance.

Moreover, there is a technical option that can be used to counter an opponent's first-strike capability. This is to put one's forces on what is called "launch on warning." A computerized tripwire would be established that would automatically launch missiles in a retaliatory strike, as soon as radar and satellite early warning systems detected incoming missiles. The enemy's missiles, instead of knocking out their targets, would hit empty silos.

Reliance on launch on warning, of course, would involve

the risk of computer malfunctions or other technical errors that could mistakenly trigger a nuclear exchange. About 150 times in the past two years, U.S. computers have mistakenly indicated a Soviet attack. In four instances, U.S. strategic forces were placed on a higher state of readiness. In one case, the rising of the moon was somehow interpreted as a Soviet missile launch. In another incident, it took six minutes to confirm that a warning of a Soviet nuclear sub attack was in fact erroneous. The timing was critical, because it only takes about fifteen minutes for their submarine-launched missile to reach the United States.

We have no reason for assuming the Soviet warning system to be less fallible than ours.

Proponents of an aggressive nuclear-war-fighting posture suggest the strategy of keeping the initial strikes limited to military targets so as to avoid major civilian casualties. Then, having disabled the enemy's forces without maiming its population, one could force the opponent to surrender or capitulate to a set of demands and hopefully avoid retaliation against one's own population.

The prospect of keeping a nuclear war limited in this way is very farfetched, however. "The niceties of targeting doctrine do not make the weapons themselves discriminating," McGeorge Bundy, former National Security Adviser in the Kennedy and Johnson administrations, said. Radioactive fallout would drift over cities and towns, causing "collateral damage" — the death and injury of countless numbers of people.

A limited nuclear attack, according to a study by the Office of Technology Assessment, would have "enormous" impact, and the "uncertainties are such that no government could predict with any confidence what the results . . . would be, even if there was no further escalation."

Once bombs start falling, it is unlikely that leaders will adhere to the well-thought-out scenarios drafted by the think-tank strategists. "Real war is not like these complicated tit-for-tat imaginings," retired Admiral Noel Gayler, former director of the National Security Agency and one-time commander of U.S.

Pacific forces, commented. "There is little knowledge of what is going on and less communication. There is blood and terror and agony."

One of the reasons for skepticism about limited nuclear war is that both the U.S. and Soviet command and control structure — government leaders, communications facilities, and military centers for coordinating a nuclear attack—are highly concentrated and thus vulnerable to attack. Once they were destroyed, centralized control over the firing of each side's nuclear weapons could be lost. John Steinbruner of the Brookings Institution estimates that 50 to 100 nuclear weapons could disrupt the central nervous system of the U.S. command structure, and a similar number could probably disable the Soviet system. Furthermore, these targets are almost certain to be among the first in an attack.

"We have to target, as discreetly as we can, the Soviet state as opposed to the Russian people," says Colin Gray, an adviser to the Departments of State and Defense. "Let's suppose there are a hundred targets, and if we could hit all these hundred targets, we'd get everyone in the Politburo, everyone in the Central Committee, we'd kill all the critically important bureaucrats, essentially we'd cut off the head of the Soviet chicken."

With the leadership "decapitated," the decision to use nuclear weapons would be scattered among hundreds of lower-level military personnel. Mr. Gray acknowledges the obvious flaw in the limited nuclear war scenarios he has advocated: "Is it sensible to destroy the government of the enemy, thus eliminating the option of negotiating an end to the war?"

Some, like Vice President George Bush, have argued that "you can have a winner" in "a nuclear exchange," even if you can't keep it limited. "The way you can have a winner," according to Bush, is to "have a capability that inflicts more damage on the opposition than it can inflict upon you." Nuclear war is survivable because "if everybody fired everything he had, you'd have more than 5 percent of the population survive."

This kind of thinking is conceivable only on an abstract,

theoretical level, far removed from the workaday world. "Think tank analysts can set levels of 'acceptable' damage well up in the hundreds of millions of lives," says McGeorge Bundy. "They are in an unreal world."

Back in the real world, people have a more sobering view of nuclear war. "If we use our 10,000 warheads, and they use their 10,000 warheads, nobody will be king," says Paul Warnke. "We could say, 'By God, we beat them—we're now ahead of the Soviet Union.' Of course, we're slightly behind the Fiji Islands."

Because of their potential for causing total annihilation, nuclear weapons cannot be treated simply as large versions of conventional weapons. Nor can they fulfill functions traditionally assigned to nonnuclear devices.

"What many Americans do not understand is that there is no sensible military use for any of the three categories of nuclear weapons—strategic, or theater, or tactical," Admiral Gayler states. "I say this as a military man, a former commander in chief of all U.S. forces in the Pacific, an aviator and mariner, soldier and intelligence officer of 46 years experience."

The United States cannot solve problems by exploding nuclear bombs: their use would lead to consequences far worse than any problem we might hope to solve. The only sensible role for these weapons is to deter others from the insanity of nuclear attack. The question to address, then, is the kind of forces we need for this narrow purpose.

We certainly do not require the kind of first-strike weapons currently under development by the Pentagon. "What really deters the Soviet Union is not the idea that we are going to destroy their ICBM silos," Richard Garwin notes, "but the idea that we can destroy their conventional military forces, their industry, their cities, and everything they have built. And you don't need highly accurate missiles to do that."

13

DUCK AND COVER

"Americans are doers. In a crisis, we'll band together and pick ourselves up by our bootstraps."
—Director, Emergency
Management Project, 1982

THE PENTAGON'S nuclear war-fighting psychology and infatuation with "limited" nuclear war scenarios are exemplified by the current program for increased civil defense preparedness.

The seven-year, $4.2 billion effort is to be carried out under the direction of the Federal Emergency Management Agency (FEMA). The premise behind the undertaking, the agency has explained, is that "the U.S. could survive a nuclear attack and go on to recovery within a relatively few years."

"Americans would not be helpless," agency representatives have argued. "They could meet and overcome all the challenges of post-attack environment" by taking protective measures such as evacuating, building fall-out shelters, and training in survival tactics.

Deputy Undersecretary of Defense, T. K. Jones, has elaborated on the effectiveness of these civil defense measures. With adequate advance preparation, he maintains, the United States could fully recover from an all-out nuclear war with the Soviet Union in two to four years. "Everybody's going to make it if there are enough shovels to go around," Jones told the *Los Angeles Times*. "Dig a hole, cover it with a couple of doors and then throw three feet of dirt on top. It's the dirt that does it."

More elaborate fall-out shelters are recommended. *Protection in the Nuclear Age,* a colorful 68-page booklet put out by FEMA, has a chapter entitled "Shelter Living," which describes a number of shelter designs, including a "snack bar" motif. To help prepare grade-school children for a nuclear attack, FEMA has also issued a special pamphlet. "Color what you would need in a shelter," it instructs. Items presented include tomatoes, crackers, beans, juice, and cake.

Not everyone would be expected to stay in their own shelter under the administration's program. FEMA is developing plans for relocating two thirds of the U.S. population in the event that nuclear war seemed unavoidable.

To help find people after a nuclear attack, FEMA has also arranged for the U.S. Post Office to prepare emergency change-of-address cards. An unintentionally disconcerting sample form, however, for Miss Mabel Jean Butler of Washington, D.C., lists her post-war address as: "Deceased, Mortuary No. 10, Falls Church, Virginia, 22040."

The administration contends that a new U.S. civil defense program is necessary to counter large-scale Soviet efforts. The alleged Russian "lead" in civil defense preparations has been cited with alarm for a number of years. A 1976 study commissioned by the CIA highlighted Soviet civil defense efforts as evidence that the Soviets were developing the capacity to fight a nuclear war, i.e., that they would put their population in shelters or evacuate them from major cities to protect against U.S. retaliation and then launch a first strike.

Short of actually starting a nuclear war, the argument continues, the Soviets could use the threat of nuclear blackmail, if they were confident they could save their populace from U.S. reprisals.

The premise behind these concerns, however, is absurd: civil defense preparations do not provide a practicable way of preventing large-scale casualties during a nuclear war. The explosion, for example, of a 1-megaton nuclear bomb at ground level would create a massive crater a half a mile across and three hundred feet deep. Like a giant hand, it would scoop out underground shelters or incinerate their inhabitants, along with everything else in the unlucky city on which it was dropped.

The shelters in an urban area struck by a number of bombs, even if left intact, would heat up like ovens, cremating the people caught inside. Those exposed to the effects of blast, radiation, and fire storms on the surface would fare no better. The availability of shelters, according to Paul Warnke, merely allows one to choose "whether you want to be fast-fried or dry-roasted."

Those managing to live through a major nuclear exchange, moreover, would find that industrial, communications, transportation, and governmental functions were completely unhinged. The survivors would be deprived of conventional supplies of food, water, shelter, and sanitary facilities. Most medical facilities would be destroyed, and medical aid would essentially be unavailable to treat the widespread burns and radiation injuries among the population.

The survivors would also face the possibility of an irreversibly damaged environment. Destruction of the stratospheric ozone layer—a potential consequence of widespread nuclear explosions—could mean the loss of much of the normal screening against the sun's ultraviolet radiation. Unless specially protected, no one could venture outdoors without risking blindness and incapacitating sunburn.

Any realistic tally of the physical damage that could be caused by the use of nuclear weapons accordingly casts grave doubts about the efficacy of the planned civil defense measures. The help they might provide would amount to a few buckets of water tossed onto an uncontrolled conflagration.

Still, the well-known facts about the effects of nuclear weapons have not dissuaded military planners, who remain convinced that Soviet civil defense efforts must be duplicated by the United States lest the "civil defense gap" remain unclosed.

Yet according to former State Department and CIA official Arthur M. Cox, the Soviets have conceded that their civil defense program would offer little protection against a U.S. nuclear attack. They merely believed it might help defend against the much smaller threat posed by China's nuclear arsenal.

The Soviet program, moreover, has never really amounted to much. The Soviets have conducted no large-scale evacuation drills; little has been done to harden industrial facilities so that they might survive an attack; new buildings are being constructed without shelters, and existing shelters generally lack stored food and water.

While the Soviets still make some effort to protect top political and military leaders, they have apparently conceded the impossibility of protecting the vast majority of their population.

Public skepticism in the U.S.S.R. about civil defense has been widespread, as the following joke, said to be circulating in Moscow, would suggest:

"Comrade, what should we do if the Americans launch a nuclear attack?"

"Wrap yourself in a sheet, and make your way slowly to the cemetery."

"Why slowly?"

"So as not to cause panic."

The acronym for their civil defense program, "grob," also happens to be the Russian word for coffin.

Public reaction in the United States to the new civil defense initiatives is similarly unenthusiastic. A typical response is that of the director of emergency planning for the city of Alexandria, Virginia, who instructed city officials not to waste time working on federal relocation plans.

It would be unwise, though, to dismiss the present civil defense program as just an overly ambitious undertaking by zealous FEMA bureaucrats. As Congressman Les Aspin observed, the plan is "extremely dangerous nonsense." For the wrongheaded idea that the country could bounce back quickly from a nuclear war, without major losses, gives great encouragement to those Pentagon planners who favor U.S. preparedness to engage in limited nuclear war.

14

THE
HIGH GROUND

"Space is a dandy arena, actually."
   —Defense Department
      scientist, 1977

THE PENTAGON has unveiled a plan to seize the ultimate military high ground from the Russians and to counter Soviet activities in outer space. Air Force Secretary Verne Orr has cautioned against putting all of our eggs in the "ground basket."

The recent Pentagon program therefore calls for efforts to wire the heavens with new nuclear-war-fighting devices, including satellite and antisatellite weapons and an updated version of the antiballistic missile (ABM) system.

The new equipment figures prominently in the drive to acquire the ability to "prevail" in a "protracted" nuclear battle with the Soviet Union. An integral part of the plan is "a vigorous and comprehensive research and development program leading to a communications and control system that would endure for an extended period beyond the first nuclear attack."

To this end, the Air Force will spend $10 to 15 billion over the next five years, outfitting satellites with gadgetry capable of monitoring a nuclear war and transmitting critical information to ground-based communications posts. These devices will warn of a nuclear attack and provide the information necessary for a coordinated response.

Defense Secretary Weinberger has also directed the Air Force to deploy antisatellite weapons within five years to counter possible Soviet breakthroughs in the development of killer satellites. Since 1968, the U.S.S.R. has been testing antisatellite weapons in space. A test was conducted as recently as June 1982. The United States has suspended antisatellite tests since 1963.

The Soviet threat to U.S. satellites is of concern because these orbiting devices provide a key means of communications, reconnaisance, navigation, and missile guidance. (A curiosity, pointed out by former weapons designer Robert Aldrich, is that "Soviet interceptor satellites are always called 'killer satellites,' while American counterparts were named SAINT—an acronym for satellite interceptor.")

Several years ago, *Aviation Week and Space Technology* reported that the Soviets had developed charged particle weapons that would be capable of destroying U.S. satellites and missiles by the early 1980s. Defense Secretary Harold Brown, a physicist by training, categorically dismissed the claim in 1977 by saying, "The laws of physics are the same in the U.S. as in the Soviet Union."

More recently, Pentagon research director Richard De-Lauer has warned that the Soviets could begin deploying laser weapons in space as early as 1983. The outlook for the 1990s, according to DeLauer, is even more dire: "We expect a large, permanent, manned orbital space complex to be operational by about 1990 . . . capable of effectively attacking . . . ground, sea, and air targets from space."

Other experts dispute this grim prediction. "It is nonsense to say the Soviets can do this as early as next year," stated a member of the Defense Science Board—a 30-member, independent advisory group to the Pentagon. The board estimates that it will take the Soviets at least ten years to develop lasers of high enough intensity to shoot down U.S. satellites. In fact, the capability may prove beyond their reach until well into the next century.

Lieutenant General Kelley Burke, Air Force chief of research, believes the Soviets might be able to launch a laser satellite in five years, but it would be "ineffective" as a weapon and would mainly serve as a propaganda tool. "I think we could do at least as well," said Burke. "The U.S. and the Soviet Union are about equal in laser technology."

Besides, space-based lasers are not very practical as weapons. They face formidable technological hurdles, not the least of which is that no one has yet succeeded in building a laser powerful enough to be an effective weapon, much less deploying it in a space vehicle. Power requirements for lasers are so high that, at current efficiencies, it would be very difficult and costly for a satellite to carry sufficient fuel to keep them operating long enough to perform useful functions.

Another problem is that if lasers were used to attack targets on or near the earth, the beams, which are influenced by atmospheric conditions, would be subject to the caprices of the weather. Aiming them with required accuracy would be a problem even in outer space.

Even if these technical difficulties are eventually overcome, defenses against lasers can still be readily devised. Lasers damage targets by causing them to overheat. A cheap and obvious countermeasure would be to put shiny surfaces on satellites or other potential targets in order to reflect the laser beam harmlessly away. The laser system may also be fooled by decoy targets.

There is a more fundamental reason that lasers make a poor choice as space weapons: there are easier and cheaper ways of destroying enemy satellites. The Air Force, for example, is currently working on a way to knock out satellites simply by arranging for another vehicle, guided by infrared sensors, to crash into them. Satellites can also be destroyed by conventional or nuclear warheads.

Richard Garwin has suggested that the United States park orbiting space mines—"little fellow travelers"—near important Soviet satellites. These simple devices could be exploded upon command.

However attractive the more exotic space weapons may be to science-fiction writers and popular moviemakers, their military potential is constrained by practical obstacles that will not easily be overcome.

15

A FLY IN
OUTER SPACE

*"A defensive policy based on deflecting attacks and pro-
tecting our citizens is just so much nicer, [but] we are just
unable to have this capability and it is no good deluding
ourselves that we can."*

Richard Garwin, 1981

A KEY ELEMENT in the ongoing enlargement of the U.S.
strategic arsenal is the development of defensive antimissile technology. Ten years have passed since the 1972 treaty that limited
ABM deployments. Research on possible ABM systems never
stopped, though, and has been stepped up over recent years by
the two superpowers. As part of the strategic modernization program, Defense Secretary Weinberger has increased the ABM
research budget by 80 percent, up to $930 million in 1983 and
$1 billion in 1984.

"We are not yet sure how well ballistic missile defenses
[BMD] will work; what they will cost; whether they would require changes to the ABM treaty; and how additional Soviet ballistic missile defenses, which would almost certainly be deployed
in response to any U.S. BMD system, would affect U.S. and
allied offensive capabilities," Weinberger told Congress.

The 1972 ABM treaty is currently up for review. Before
jeopardizing one of the few and very important achievements

in the history of arms negotiations, it is worth determining whether the advantages of deploying a missile defense system outweigh the risks of the inevitable escalation in arms competition.

An ideal ballistic missile defense system would, in theory, eliminate the threat of nuclear bombs exploding on American soil. Taken in the abstract, it is an attractive idea.

Lieutenant General Daniel Graham compares a space-based missile defense system to having "a screen of, say, cavalry out in front of you. Certainly cavalry now aren't invulnerable to the other side's weapons, but they create a situation where you have to fight through a defense" before you can attack the main targets. Neither side has any such defense today.

The obvious question is whether ballistic missile defense is, in fact, feasible. After all, the earlier ABM was abandoned by both sides in 1972 primarily because it did not work. It is not clear that things have changed all that much since then.

Professor Jack Ruina of the Massachusetts Institute of Technology, former director of advanced research at the Pentagon, maintains that "given the advances in offensive technology, we are no closer to being able to design an effective system for the defense of cities and industry than we were a decade ago." Nor have the Soviets achieved any breakthrough in BMD technology. Khrushchev's old claim that they "could hit a fly in outer space" is as empty a boast today as it was twenty years ago.

The use of lasers to shoot down missiles, for example, faces problems similar to those involved in shooting down satellites. Charles Townes, the Nobel Prize–winning physicist, considers the use of lasers against missiles "a science fiction idea at the moment. It's a glamorous kind of thing that everyone wants to believe will work, but it's very much overblown."

It may be possible, in principle, to design a laser capable of destroying an ICBM after it has been launched. The practical difficulties, however, in designing a system able to intercept hundreds of missiles simultaneously appear insurmountable at present.

"The history of BMD development is replete with instances in which simple countermeasures, *sure* to be deployed by the time we could build a BMD, were ignored, while vast expenditures and promises were made for the performance of the system," Richard Garwin observed. A U.S. BMD, he concludes, "won't work. That is, unless the Soviet Union goes out of its way to help us make it work."

As with satellites, one countermeasure would be to coat the missiles with shiny aluminum. This would increase energy requirements for the laser by a factor of twenty, Garwin estimates. He also suggests the possibility of enclosing nuclear reentry vehicles in aluminum-foil balloons and then sending up thousands of indistinguishable decoy balloons.

Another practical problem would arise in the deployment of a space-based BMD. Neither side is likely to sit back and do nothing while the other side goes about building such a system. The temptation would be strong for the other side to destroy the BMD during early stages of construction.

Even if one succeeded in getting such a system in place, it would at best be able to protect only a selected number of missile bases. It could never ensure blanket protection of U.S. cities, where only a few warheads slipping through would mean disaster. The Soviets could always deploy enough offensive weapons to overwhelm any defense we might muster and vice versa. Nor could the system offer any protection against cruise missiles or other nuclear delivery vehicles that stayed within the atmosphere.

The BMD complex itself would be highly vulnerable to attack. The Soviets could incapacitate the system by destroying its radar directly, or they could "blind" it, along with other solid-state electronic equipment in the continental United States, with the electromagnetic pulse produced by detonating a large nuclear bomb high in the atmosphere.

There is also the possibility that a BMD might defeat itself. Some proposed systems would employ thousands of nuclear-armed interceptor missiles whose explosions might black out their own radar.

A further practical consideration is that the costs of such a system would be staggering, estimated in the hundreds of billions of dollars. These costs would increase considerably if the Soviet Union takes advantage of simple ways of foiling the laser attacks, which they are certain to do.

In sum, the United States *could* try to build a BMD, but it is questionable what benefits would be derived from doing so. Thomas Reed, former Secretary of the Air Force, led a special review in 1981 of BMD technology for the Defense Science Board. A BMD program, he concluded, was not worth the enormous effort and expense it would require.

16

LIGHTING FUSES

"Missiles will bring anti-missiles, and anti-missiles will bring anti-anti-missiles. But inevitably, this whole electronic house of cards will reach a point where it can be constructed no higher."

—*General Omar N. Bradley,*
1957

NEWTON'S THIRD LAW says that for every force there is an equal and opposite force. In the nuclear arms race, there is a similar principle: for every action taken by one side there will be an inevitable reaction by the other. U.S. and Soviet military planners, however, frequently overlook this basic principle. They tend to examine proposed strategic weapons only very narrowly to determine whether they will provide a great advance in destructive power or accuracy. If the answer is yes and the apparent advantage sufficiently large, they then proceed to develop and deploy the new wonder weapon. The United States, with its lead in military technology, has repeatedly rushed to capitalize on every major new technological possibility. Little attention is paid to likely Soviet responses.

"Too often our technologists say, 'Let's not worry about counter-measures. Maybe the Soviets won't think of it and, anyhow, it's more fun to develop new systems,' " Richard Garwin, who has had years of firsthand experience as a senior adviser to the Pentagon, observed.

Mimicking the U.S. advance or setting out to develop comparable technology, as the Soviets have repeatedly done, is the most obvious response.

It seems that "the U.S. is racing with itself," Jerome Wiesner, science adviser to President Kennedy, commented. "The Soviets are pretty good at following... We see a reflection of our best ideas in what the Soviets do."

The habitual official neglect of likely Soviet reactions was brought home to us in a conversation with a senior Air Force officer who was working on plans for the MX missile. After listening to his description of the merits of the new missile, we asked, "What do you expect the Soviets to do if we deploy the MX?"

The question, which was followed by a long pause, finally produced the reply that he didn't know, but whatever they did, we'd then respond appropriately.

The Air Force, it has become clear, has focused almost exclusively on the short-term advantages of the MX missile without thinking through the full implications of deploying it. Had the Air Force done so, it would have realized that the Soviets could counter a U.S. MX in a number of ways.

The Soviets, as noted earlier, could build more warheads to try to overwhelm the MX, and they could offset its first-strike potential by programing their own ICBMs to launch on warning. They could also deploy their own mobile ICBMs and play the same game of hide-and-seek in Siberia that the U.S. Air Force proposed for Utah and Nevada.

Thus, it ought to be clear by this point in the arms race that technology alone cannot secure a decisive strategic advantage for either side. By the time America can develop a ballistic missile defense system capable of killing ICBMs in flight, for example, the Soviets would be very likely to come up with suitable countermeasures. This country will then have to spend more time and money developing countercounter measures, and on and on it will go.

One area where the United States currently has a clear

technical lead is cruise missiles—small self-guided and self-propelled aircraft that can deliver either conventional or nuclear warheads. Current plans call for deploying about 4,000 of these missiles on bombers, submarines, and ground-based launchers starting late in 1983. To date, none of the arms control proposals put forward by the U.S. would interfere with these plans.

The introduction of cruise missiles, like other such advances, will light another fuse in the arms race, for it will inspire a corresponding Soviet effort. The new missiles themselves are very small—as little as 14 feet long and 2 feet wide—and can be concealed on planes, ships, and even trucks.

The Navy plans to install hundreds of them on its general-purpose submarines—a plan that is ill advised when likely Soviet countermoves are taken into consideration. Because cruise missiles are so easily hidden, neither the United States nor the Soviets could be certain of how many of them the other side has. Nor could either side tell whether its opponent's cruise missiles were armed with nuclear or conventional warheads. The widespread deployment of cruise missiles would, therefore, jeopardize future hopes for nuclear arms control, which is based on numerical limits on weapons that can be verified by counting.

"If we go ahead with sea-launched cruise, we can know that the Soviets will," Paul Warnke cautions. "We'd have to consider every Soviet fishing vessel as a potential strategic delivery vehicle. You wouldn't know whether it was full of codfish or cruise missiles."

By proceeding with the cruise, we will repeat the mistake made in the early 1970s, when we refused to sacrifice our temporary lead in MIRV technology. Now is the time to forestall the introduction of these missiles, before the Soviet Union develops them and before the United States deploys them.

A U.S. lead in cruise—or any other weapons—technology is bound to be short-lived. If we somehow manage to get ahead, the Soviets will devote whatever resources necessary to catch up. "The Soviet Union is fully resolved not to fall behind the U.S.," maintains Henry Trofimenko of the Soviet Academy of Sciences. History, to date, has validated this claim.

The United States, however, seems to be counting on a

strategy of exhausting the Soviets. We'll outrun them with a heroic effort in the next several years to develop new weapons, and when they're worn out from arms competition, they will supposedly agree to end the arms race on our terms.

"What we're trying to do is dictate their investment strategy," Pentagon scientist Richard DeLauer has stated. "Then maybe they'll sit down and take the President seriously and talk about reducing the numbers, which is the whole damn purpose of the exercise."

This is foolishness, since the kind of countermeasures the Soviet Union could employ need not be very expensive or technically sophisticated. The Soviets could thus defeat a hundred-billion-dollar U.S. laser-shooting BMD by the relatively cheap and easy method of putting shiny coatings on their missiles.

There are other, more worrisome responses to the kind of first-strike capability the Pentagon is striving to attain. "The U.S.S.R. can't match the U.S. missile for missile," a Soviet official has explained. "We can't do it economically. But we don't have to be a mirror . . . The more you have in counterforce capability, the more there is the danger that the other side will build up and go to a launch-on-warning, with the computer element stepped up and the human element reduced. And of course, that's more dangerous."

The further political assumption, that the Soviets would agree to quit the arms race while the United States had some major lead in technology of numbers, is similarly hard to believe.

"We know we're not going to give up, and we have no reason to believe they will," Paul Warnke says. "All you will do is to preserve the present nuclear stalemate at higher levels of risk."

A telling insight into the dynamics of the arms race was given recently by former Secretary of Defense Robert McNamara. "I have no doubt that the Soviets thought we were trying to achieve a first-strike capability," he observed. "If I had been the Soviet secretary of defense [in the 1960s], I'd have been worried as hell. . . ." "The way they [the Soviets] reacted," he added, "was by substantially expanding their strategic nuclear weapons program . . . So you have an action-reaction phenomenon. And the result is that during the last 25 years, and particularly during the last 15, there has been a large buildup . . . in the nuclear strength of these two forces. That has changed the nature of the problem and increased the risk greatly."

Clearly, ample precedents suggest that the new strategic buildup recently begun by the United States, with its emphasis on first-strike weaponry, will automatically trigger a frantic expansion of the already overheated arms race with the U.S.S.R.

PART III

THE WAY OUT

17

THE SEARCH
FOR SOLUTIONS

*"The unleashed power of the atom has changed everything
save our modes of thinking, and we thus drift toward un-
paralleled catastrophes."*
                                    —*Albert Einstein, 1946*

A DOCTOR is called in, at the eleventh hour, to treat a patient
suffering from an advanced, life-threatening disease. The danger
to the patient's life is apparent; the cure is not. As he studies the
case, the doctor sees no wound that can be cleansed with simple
disinfectants. He finds no localized tumor that can be excised
with deft surgery. He is unable to recommend a wonder drug as
the obvious palliative. He learns that even the latest and most
advanced medical technology is of little help. The case involves
a complicated, systemic illness. Its treatment will require supreme ingenuity, heroic efforts, and much patience.

The nuclear arms race, in many ways, is like this disease,
for it, too, lacks simple origins and defies simple cures. It has
gone on for so long, and has involved such an extraordinary set
of factors—political, military, bureaucratic, and technological—
that any antidote is extremely difficult to prescribe.

There is no prospect, moreover, that a wise outsider, a re-
nowned specialist, can be called in to work a miracle cure. The
two superpowers, who suffer a disease of their own making, have

to find the solution themselves. This will be all the harder because they must grapple not just with each other but also with their own warped perceptions.

Cold war paranoia still influences the leaders and military establishments on both sides. Each country exaggerates the size of the other's military forces. Each takes the blackest possible view of the other's motivations. Each is obsessed with grossly implausible scenarios of surprise attacks by the other. Each is unwilling to cede any potential advantage to its rival.

These attitudes—the psychosomatic contributors to the cancerous growth of the U.S. and Soviet nuclear arsenals—have to be altered if nuclear war is to be avoided. Each side, in the end, will have to free itself from various myths, the greatest delusion of all being that it still has something to gain from a continuing buildup of nuclear weaponry.

Psychological problems are not the only complications, however. Despite the unbalanced view the superpowers take of the threats to their national security, each still faces a genuine challenge from the other. Even paranoids can have real enemies: their problem is that they cannot distinguish actual from imagined dangers.

As much as the United States fears nuclear war, it also fears not having enough nuclear weapons to thwart the Soviet Union from encroaching on its vital interests. The underlying national security concern is wholly legitimate.

"Getting rid of all nuclear weapons," accordingly, is not a practical solution that either superpower could consider. Unlike a virus that one wants to rid from the body, nuclear weapons cannot be so easily disposed of. They have served the United States, and will continue to serve for the foreseeable future, as a principal means of coping with the threat posed by the U.S.S.R. The Soviets, similarly, rely on nuclear weapons to protect what they regard as their vital interests.

The path to nuclear sanity, therefore, will not be a short, straight road to a nuclear-free world. It will require both sides to devise a solution to a twofold problem: how to avoid nuclear war *and* how to maintain national security.

The superpowers must ultimately go to the bargaining table if they are to work out a satisfactory denouement to the arms race. They have been sitting down, off and on, for years, and a salient feature of their discussions is the amount of time consumed.

The SALT I Treaty took three years to negotiate; SALT II took seven, but was left unratified by the Senate as a result of the Soviet invasion of Afghanistan. It was then set aside by the Reagan administration, which wanted a revised arrangement. More than a year and a half passed before renewed negotiations began. Their duration will be anybody's guess.

The manufacture of nuclear bombs and the development of new weapons systems, in contrast, are fast-paced. By the time diplomats have agreed on limits to one set of weapons, other more sophisticated ones are already being tested and readied for deployment.

The political process has to catch up with the technology if the arms race is to be stopped. This will not happen unless the superpowers recognize the fundamental truths about security in the nuclear age. Five basic premises, at a minimum, must be accepted by the two nations if their negotiations are to be productive.

First, both sides maintain nuclear arsenals that are essentially equivalent in destructive power. They have long since achieved the only realistic objective of arming themselves with nuclear weapons: a secure deterrent against nuclear attack. Beyond that, there is nothing that either superpower can reasonably hope to gain by enlarging its nuclear stockpile. Additional pieces of nuclear ordnance, however destructive or sophisticated they might be, would convey no usable military advantage: they would be just so many more matches thrown into the fire storms ignited by existing nuclear bombs.

Second, there is nothing but a vain hope of achieving a technological "breakthrough" that would give one side the upper hand. The only conceivable technological development that would matter much would be the perfection of a defense against nuclear attack: the invention, say, of some umbrella the size of a continent that could prevent nuclear warheads from raining down from the sky onto their targets.

Modern science and engineering can perform great feats, but not miracles, which is essentially what it would take to blunt the devastating force of a concerted nuclear attack. The best scientific minds in each country have searched, for decades, for the magic that would deflect or destroy incoming nuclear bombs, but they have pitifully little to show for their efforts. Improvements in offensive nuclear weapons have so far outpaced defensive efforts, and the experts offer no hope that a panacea will soon be within their grasp. Neither side, accordingly, can "win" the arms race, no matter how strenuously it might try.

Third, the arms race verges on a new, more dangerous cycle of technological competition. Both sides are developing weaponry that will give them a potential first-strike capability against the other's ICBMs. In a time of crisis, such weaponry might create the incentive for preemptive strikes. It may also force the two nations to rely on computers programmed to launch on warning, as the Soviets have already hinted they may do. The chances of war by miscalculation, or electronic error, will increase dramatically as deployment of first-strike weapons proceeds.

Other technological advances—such as the development and deployment of space weapons and cruise missiles—also threaten to create a heightened arms race in the 1980s that will be difficult, perhaps impossible, to control. For the side that lags behind will inevitably refuse to terminate the race while it is behind; its efforts to catch up, of course, will inevitably provoke the pace setter to make even greater strides.

Given the present parity in their nuclear forces, both sides now face what may be their last chance to halt the arms race before a new, more perilous stage in their perennial competition gets started.

Fourth, both sides have such large and diverse nuclear arsenals—such massive "overkill" in assured destructive capability—that they have considerable negotiating flexibility. Secure about their deterrent, they can approach the bargaining table without feeling hysterical about the need to hold on to every last bomb they have. They can even feel confident about making drastic reductions in their arsenals while still maintaining adequate nuclear strength.

Nor need the two nations worry excessively about what had been the central obstacle to early arms control proposals: the fear of cheating by one side. When both sides had small or modest nuclear arsenals, the clandestine manufacture of a small number of weapons by one side could make a large difference. With mammoth arsenals, the danger diminishes. Even major violations of agreed-upon limits—which would, in any event, be difficult to conceal—would be of minor consequence militarily (although politically devastating). A thousand nuclear bombs secretly produced in the 1950s or early 1960s might have given one side an overwhelming nuclear edge; today, another thousand bombs would count as much to either superpower as the small change in a rich man's pocket.

Fifth, the two nations must be willing to abandon their pursuit of new weapons systems. Any agreement that limited the number of weapons, but permitted an ongoing and vigorous weapons-development process, would fail to cut the arms race off at its roots. For it is the dramatic advances in technology such as those which confer theoretical first-strike capability—rather than the mere number of nuclear bombs—that constitute the greatest source of danger in a runaway arms race.

Giving up a lead or potential lead in new weapons technology is what neither side, pursuing its narrow interest, would want to do. Still, no agreement intended to end the arms race will last, in the long run, if either side feels disadvantaged and thus compelled to catch up with the other.

"So far as nuclear war is concerned, we and the Soviet Union are in the same boat," Professor Roger Fisher of the Harvard Law School observed. "You can think of that physically. There is no way that we can make our end of the boat safer by making the other end more likely to tip over."

To end the nuclear arms race once and for all, both sides must be willing to forgo short-run advantages to achieve the broader common goal of avoiding nuclear war. If they can so change their "modes of thinking," to use Einstein's phrase, by keeping in mind the premises that must guide productive negotiations, their search for alternatives to a continuing weapons buildup will be dramatically enhanced.

18

ENDGAME

*"People want peace so much that government had better
get out of their way and let them have it."*
—*Dwight Eisenhower,
1960*

NEGOTIATING a major international treaty can involve numberless details.

Each side, on its own whim, can choose to dispute every conceivable issue, all the way from the shape of the conference table to the most sweeping political accommodations. The attitude of the participants will determine whether the talks get sidetracked by trivia or proceed expeditiously toward a definitive agreement.

Ideally, the United States and U.S.S.R. would both come to the bargaining table prepared to act rationally to secure their long-run national interests. Aware of the risks in continuing the nuclear arms race, they would take bold steps to end this dangerously overheated competition.

Looking at their situation objectively, they would ideally also recognize that it is not just head-on superpower confrontations that carry the danger of nuclear war. Conventional wars can also entangle the two nations and grow into nuclear conflicts. This risk must be greatly reduced. Accordingly, the two nations would discuss the many particular issues that have brought them into conflict around the world and then try to develop means to help keep the peace between them. They would conclude that their common interest in avoiding nuclear war transcends their other priorities.

Were a broad peace-keeping arrangement adopted, it would include what General Bernard Rogers, the Supreme Allied Commander in Europe, calls "a comprehensive array of equitable and verifiable arms reduction accords and arms control measures which can lead to reduced and balanced levels for *all* categories of forces."

This kind of treaty is surely a utopian goal, however, so long as the superpowers retain their cold war mentality. It is so difficult to get the two nations to talk that the leap toward a general peace treaty, as rational a step as it might be, seems a long way off. For the present, the priority must be placed on finding some satisfactory first step—some way of breaking the ice—that will put them on a path to nuclear sanity.

The nuclear freeze proposal—a ban on the buildup of nuclear weapons along with a ban on the testing of nuclear bombs and new delivery systems—is just such a measure.

The way to end the nuclear arms race, to borrow the late senator Thomas Aiken's proposal for terminating the Vietnam war, is for each side to declare itself the winner and just stop racing.

This is not a wholly facetious suggestion, and it is the basic idea behind a bilateral nuclear freeze. However simplistic the freeze might at first appear, it is entirely consistent with the basic considerations that must govern a satisfactory arms control agreement between the United States and the U.S.S.R. It offers many strong advantages for both sides.

First, a freeze at the current level of nuclear armaments would be equitable to both countries, whose strategic forces are essentially equivalent in size and destructive power. It would leave them both with a secure deterrent capability.

Second, the freeze would prevent the deployment by both

sides of new weapons, now under development, that would have a possible first-strike capability against the other side's ICBMs. This would bring a swift halt to the single greatest threat to the stability of the nuclear balance.

A freeze would also prevent the widespread deployment of cruise missiles by both sides. If this is not done now, it might never be done, because once these small, easily hidden missiles are deployed in large numbers, a verifiable arms control treaty that limits them will be very difficult, if not impossible, to effect.

Third, the freeze would halt plans that would dramatically escalate the arms race by placing nuclear war-fighting systems in outer space.

Fourth, a freeze would embody one of the most sought-after arms-control goals: a comprehensive ban on the testing of new nuclear warheads and delivery systems. Indeed, this is perhaps the most important aspect of the freeze, more significant than a mere cap on the number of warheads and delivery vehicles. For without testing, there can be no deployment of new, more exotic weapons because no one would be sure they could work. Hence, the main force that propels the arms race forward, the uncontrolled process of technological innovation, would be blunted decisively.

Extensive U.S.-Soviet negotiations have been held on a "comprehensive test ban" but they were suspended by President Carter in 1980 and, in July 1982, the Reagan administration decided against resuming talks on this subject. Resumption and consumation of the negotiations, however, are a critical element in achieving a satisfactory freeze.

Fifth, both sides could adopt a freeze with confidence that such an agreement could be adequately verified. Present U.S. satellite reconnaissance capability, for example, would swiftly disclose the deployment or test-firing of new Soviet missiles. We have also improved our ability to detect underground tests of even small nuclear bombs and to distinguish the shock waves they create from those of earthquakes.

A further basis for confidence in the ability to check compliance with the freeze has been the U.S. experience in monitoring past arms control agreements with the U.S.S.R. Our verification systems, according to Senator Daniel P. Moynihan, vice chairman of the Senate Select Committee on Intelligence, "give us high levels of confidence that the Soviets have been in general compliance with SALT I and, so far, with the SALT II agreement as well."

A 1979 State Department report on alleged Soviet violations of SALT found that "in each case the U.S. has raised, the action in question has either ceased or additional information has allayed our concern."

The United States will monitor military developments in the Soviet Union regardless of whether there is an arms control agreement. A complete ban on the critical aspects of weapons development, however, would be much easier to verify than a complicated treaty like SALT II that imposes numerical ceilings on various weapons systems.

"Since a freeze would mean a stop to all activities in any weapons programs, the detection of even one missile or bomber would be evidence of a violation," former CIA Deputy Director Herbert Scoville points out. For example, a ceiling on highly portable cruise missiles would be hard to monitor, because one could never be certain whether a specific missile fell within the permitted quota. On the other hand, "a total ban on testing, production, and deployment could be checked with high confidence," Scoville adds.

A major advantage of a freeze is that it can be effected by both sides without protracted negotiations. It does not require haggling over complex numerical limits and can be adopted promptly if the two nations so choose.

So deadlocked are the two nations, however, that it may take a very bold gesture to dispel the mutual mistrust that keeps the arms race going. To induce the U.S.S.R. to participate in a freeze the United States might unilaterally adopt a moratorium on weapons deployment and testing and challenge the Soviets to follow suit. (In 1977, more than 12,000 scientists, engineers, and other professionals, under the auspices of the Union of Concerned Scientists, made such a recommendation.) The United

States, after all, has been the technological leader in virtually every stage of the arms race, and has introduced the major innovations. Couldn't we try to lead the way out of the process?

The United States could, for example, declare its intention to freeze deployment and testing of nuclear weapons as of such and such a date, if the Soviet Union would follow suit. The Soviet Union, of course, could announce its own freeze and challenge the United States to do the same.

"I am convinced that Soviet leaders, young and old, desire serious negotiations," W. Averell Harriman, former U.S. Ambassador to the U.S.S.R., states. Although you can't count on the Russians to act in our interest, Harriman added, "you can trust the Russians to act in the Russian interest." They are presumably as anxious to stop U.S. deployment of MX missiles, Trident II submarines, and cruise missiles as we are to curtail further deployment of Soviet SS–20 missiles, Typhoon submarines, and Backfire bombers.

If this is indeed a correct description of Soviet intentions, there could be no more persuasive way of demonstrating it to the United States than an announcement of a Soviet nuclear freeze.

Whichever side takes the initiative and makes the historic gesture to end the arms race, it can only be hoped that it does so soon. For as Britain's Lord Zuckerman observes, "With every delay in reaching an agreement on the control of nuclear arms, nuclear weapons change and build up so fast that the best that can be achieved later is worse than the worst that might have been concluded a year or two ago."

19

WINDING DOWN

"Is it possible to break out of this charmed and vicious circle?"

—*George Kennan,*
1981

ON SOME of the treacherous roads high in the Colorado Rockies, there is nothing between the narrow roadway and a drop of thousands of feet. One hairpin turn follows another, but in many places there are few precise warning signs. Instead, from time to time, drivers will see at the outer edge of a precipice a simple placard that just says, "THINK!"

The United States and the U.S.S.R. have been racing faster and faster up such a winding mountain road. The chasm into which they risk falling has been getting deeper and deeper. They have kept going, heedless of the increasing danger, trying to pass each other despite the chance of skidding off together into the thermonuclear abyss. The two nations must finally "THINK!" and appreciate the urgency of stopping their insanely dangerous race.

Still, a step such as a freeze in the buildup of nuclear arms, however welcome a sign of newfound sanity, will hardly eliminate the risk of nuclear war. Although no longer trying to pass each other, the superpowers will remain high up on the narrow

94

mountain road. A mistake or miscalculation could push them over the edge. For the nuclear arsenals they currently maintain, even if not a single bomb is added to them, can be used to obliterate each other many times over.

The two countries must therefore do more than just halt the arms race. They must work to build a stable peace. They will have to carefully turn themselves around, reduce their nuclear arsenals, and start slowly back down the steep road. Their goal must be to reduce the chances of nuclear war as much as possible and to scale down the level of destructiveness that such a conflict might entail.

Were the two countries simply to freeze their nuclear arsenals at present levels and do nothing else, it might prove difficult to sustain such an arrangement. The pressures that have driven the superpowers to accumulate advanced weaponry are very strong. These pent-up forces—many of which derive from cold war suspicions and the expansionary tendencies of military bureaucracies—could, over time, tempt both sides to compromise what might come to be regarded only as a "temporary" freeze. This, after all, happened before, when both sides abandoned the moratorium on nuclear testing they had agreed upon in 1958.

If an end to the arms race is to become permanent, the United States and the U.S.S.R. must work to reduce the suspicions that have driven them to compete so frantically with each other. They have worked for years to reinforce the "credibility" of their deterrents—their willingness to use nuclear weapons. To end the arms race once and for all, both sides must work to reinforce the credibility of their commitments to accept agreed-upon limits.

The most convincing evidence of the two superpowers' intention to forswear future arms buildups would be their willingness to make actual reductions in existing nuclear stockpiles. Each round of weapons cuts will be a confidence-building exercise; the culmination of several such rounds will be a world with drastically reduced nuclear arsenals and a drastically reduced chance that those that remain will ever be used.

Complete disarmament, however, is not a presently realistic goal. Even if all nuclear weapons could be destroyed, the knowledge of how to build them would not be eliminated, and thus the threat would still remain. "The genie is out of the bottle," Vice Admiral John Lee commented. "There is no way to regain nuclear virginity."

There is also no practical alternative, at present, to the concept of deterring nuclear war by maintaining an adequate retaliatory capability. Although the two nations must come down off the dangerous mountain precipice, they will not reach sea level: a world with no nuclear weapons. They will instead reach something like the Colorado Plateau, in which they both maintain nuclear arsenals adequate for deterrence, but very much smaller than those they presently have.

With combined strategic arsenals of about 17,000 nuclear bombs, equivalent to 1,000,000 Hiroshimas in killing power, both sides clearly have more nuclear bombs than they need. The major question, then, is how many weapons are needed to deter a potential attacker.

About 25 percent of the Soviet population and 50 percent of its industry is concentrated in the country's 100 largest cities. One hundred well-placed bombs would therefore inflict unprecedented devastation. Allowing for misfires and inaccuracies, far fewer than 1,000 secure and reliable bombs would provide a very adequate deterrent.

This estimate is similar to one made by Secretary of Defense Robert McNamara in the 1960s. The United States, he concluded, would need only about 400 one-megaton bombs—with a total power of 30,000 Hiroshimas—to maintain an adequate deterrent. Beyond that, Pentagon analysts believed the United States would face "the fact of strongly diminishing marginal returns," i.e., it would just waste money in building more bombs once it already had enough.

This country, therefore, does not require large numbers of increasingly exotic weapons to make an attack against it an insane step by the Soviet Union; it merely needs a small fraction of the bombs it already has to carry out the mission of deterrence.

The United States could, for example, maintain an arsenal closer in size to that of Britain and France, which together have a total of about 700 nuclear bombs. Britain has 4 submarines, with 16 missiles (each with 3 warheads) that can hit the U.S.S.R. It also has 56 Vulcan bombers. France has 18 intermediate-range missiles, 70 bombers, and five subs (each equipped with 16 missiles). The total destructive force represented by their arsenals is equivalent to about 10,000 Hiroshimas.

The Soviet Union, like the United States, only needs a small fraction of its present nuclear arsenal to inflict enough damage to feel confident that it can deter any strike against it.

How do the superpowers go about reducing their swollen nuclear arsenals to the modest levels needed to maintain adequate deterrence?

An initial goal, suggested by George Kennan, former U.S. Ambassador to the Soviet Union, would be an across-the-board 50 percent reduction in U.S. and Soviet stockpiles "without further wrangling among the experts." Given the massive levels of overkill in current arsenals, this is something both sides can safely afford to do. Even after dismantling and destroying thousands of nuclear weapons, each side would still be left with destructive power equal to several hundred thousand Hiroshimas. Their arsenals could be reduced further by a series of equal, verifiable cutbacks.

It is not so much the percentage that counts in the initial reductions, however. What is critical is that the process of reducing current arsenals get started. A prompt 5 to 10 percent reduction "without further wrangling among the experts" would do more to counter the momentum of the arms race than open-ended negotiations aimed at more ambitious cutbacks.

In addition to reducing the overall number of nuclear weapons in their stockpiles, the United States and U.S.S.R. could profitably explore the possibility of more selective reductions. Some nuclear weapons are more dangerous than others. This is so not just because some have greater explosive yield, but because they possess technical features that cause special problems. Chief among the latter are those weapons that have the potential for a first strike against the other side's ICBMs.

The United States and the U.S.S.R., to reduce the fears of a first strike, could negotiate a major tradeoff: each side would eliminate an agreed-upon number of its most accurate ICBMs. The United States, with its large number of submarine-launched missiles, could even consider getting rid of many or all of its land-based ICBMs in exchange for major Soviet concessions. Shifting to a submarine-based deterrent would have major advantages for the United States: it would eliminate the potential first-strike threat against ICBMs that has been of such great concern and it would make the continental United States much less of a potential military target.

As the negotiating process continued, other positive steps could also be considered. For example:

• the 1972 ABM agreement, which is now up for review, could be kept in effect in order to continue the ban on deployment of ballistic missile defense systems

• anti-satellite weapons could be banned, alleviating growing concerns that vital command and communications links and early warning systems could be cut by either side

• a ban on production of hunter-killer submarines and on the deployment of devices for antisubmarine warfare could be adopted that would give both sides much greater peace of mind about the future security of their submarine-based portion of their deterrent

• a jointly manned communications center could be established to help reduce the risk that a nuclear war might start by accident

Thus, once the United States and the U.S.S.R. decide to abandon their dangerous perch atop the mountain of thermonuclear explosives they have built, they will find no shortage of good ideas for establishing a more stable peace between them.

20

NO FIRST USE

"When they talk of a limited nuclear war, they mean limited to us."

> —Chairman of the British Labour Party,
> 1981

WORLD WAR I began in Europe. World War II began in Europe. World War III, if it comes, may start there as well. The United States and the Soviet Union, as a result of the NATO and Warsaw Pact alliances, come into their most direct confrontation on that continent. It is the most heavily armed region in the world.

The Soviet Union, which lost 20 million people in World War II, is obsessed by the need to defend itself against another attack from the West, and from Germany in particular. A long history of earlier invasions reinforces Russian anxieties. The U.S. alliance with Germany is deeply disturbing to them. The Soviet buildup of allegedly defensive forces in Eastern Europe, on the other hand, raises concern in the West, where the Soviet conquest of that region after World War II is also not forgotten.

Because of the size and power of Soviet conventional forces, the United States and its NATO allies have depended for the last three decades on U.S. nuclear weapons to deter an attack on Europe. This policy was originally adopted when Europe, devastated by World War II, was unable to match the Red Army. The United States had a big early lead in nuclear weaponry over the U.S.S.R. and therefore extended a nuclear "umbrella" over the continent. A further reason for offering this special protection was that the United States did not want Germany to seek its own nuclear weapons. This consideration, which is still a factor in the thinking of U.S. officials, is politely left unspoken today.

The United States has some 900 military installations in Western Europe, and it has deployed 6,000 "theater" nuclear weapons that are ready for use on the continent. These encompass everything from nuclear land mines and artillery shells up to short-range missiles. The United States has also assigned bombers to NATO and put nuclear subs on patrol in European waters. The Soviets, who have long since closed the gap with the United States in strategic nuclear weapons (that is, weapons of intercontinental range), have also built up an arsenal of about 4,500 short-range tactical nuclear weapons for possible use in a European conflict.

No plausible scenario for an unprovoked Soviet attack on Western Europe has been developed; still, the theoretical possibility of such a move remains a principal element behind NATO's planning. There is also the concern that some kind of crisis in Eastern Europe might develop into a major struggle between NATO and the Warsaw Pact in the course of which the Soviets might invade.

An expansion of the nuclear forces on both sides is currently underway. The Soviet Union has deployed about 250 mobile SS-20 missiles with triple warheads in Europe. (These missiles threaten cities and military installations in Western Europe, but lack the range to hit targets in the United States.)

In December 1979, at the request of NATO, the United States agreed to deploy additional nuclear weapons in Europe. Beginning in 1983, 108 Pershing–2 ballistic missiles and 464 Tomahawk cruise missiles are scheduled to be stationed there under U.S. control. Unlike the bulk of current NATO nuclear weapons, which have a range of less than a few dozen miles, both the Pershings and the cruise missiles will have the capability to attack Moscow and other targets in the Soviet heartland. A Pershing–2 launched from Germany would reach the Soviet capital in six minutes.

The NATO plan has met with intense public opposition in Europe. The new land-based missiles, which the host countries would not control, raise the specter of a U.S.-Soviet duel on European soil, with the new missiles as both the prime weapons and the prime targets of such a frightening exercise.

Mass demonstrations in European capitals have been held to protest the installation of the new U.S. missiles. In response to the growing strain on the NATO alliance, President Reagan made an alternate proposal in November 1981. Under his "zero option" plan, the United States would not deploy the Pershing–2s and Tomahawk missiles if the Soviet Union would dismantle all 600 of its intermediate-range missiles—SS–20s and the older SS–4s and SS–5s.

The Soviet Union was not eager to scrap existing missiles for ones the United States might not, in any event, even be able to deploy because of European political opposition. Soviet Premier Brezhnev responded, in February 1982, with a counter-proposal that both the United States and U.S.S.R. agree to add no more weapons to the NATO and Warsaw Pact nuclear stockpiles. Negotiations on the subject are now underway.

In terms of a concrete military threat to NATO, it should be immediately apparent that the Soviet SS–20s do not create a particularly *new* problem. The Soviets have had such a large strategic arsenal that it has long been within their power to devastate Europe. They could do so easily, almost as a backhand gesture. It is irrelevant which part of their arsenal—long-range strategic weapons or shorter-range weapons—they would use for such an attack. The consequences to Europe would be the same.

Since 1963, the Soviet Union has had a virtual monopoly on intermediate-range missiles, but this has mattered little to NATO, which has had a deterrent force that relies heavily on submarine-launched missiles and bombers. Both sides have arsenals that are comparable in overall nuclear firepower. It has been this bottom-line consideration, not the type of delivery vehicle used by each side, that has maintained mutual deterrence.

The United States and NATO, however, feel that the new land-based missiles are necessary, in part, because of their symbolic value. As Assistant Secretary of Defense Richard Perle has explained, "Forces seen on land in Europe have an inherent credibility that forces more distant and invisible can't match."

The Soviets, nevertheless, presumably know that their citizens killed by a warhead from an "invisible" NATO submarine will be just as dead as those killed by a Pershing–2. It is unclear how the latter has any more "credibility" as a deterrent. If they do not think we will use the weapons we have, why should they think we will use the new ones?

The most critical issue about U.S. nuclear weapons in Europe is not their kind or number but the overall strategy for their use. The long-standing NATO posture—adopted when the Soviets had a small nuclear arsenal and NATO did not have its present strength in conventional forces—has been to threaten to use nuclear weapons in the event that NATO forces fail to repel a conventional Soviet attack.

Implicit in NATO's "first use" doctrine is the notion of "flexible response," under which tactical nuclear weapons can supposedly be used in a controlled way, gradually moving up the "ladder of escalation," without necessarily precipitating all-out nuclear war.

The official thinking is, at best, confused. There is no agreement on precisely what constitutes a "tactical" weapon (although cynics have defined it as "one that blows up in Europe"). There is also no real understanding of how a nuclear war, once started, would be kept under control. War has never been a politely choreographed exercise in which the belligerents behave with impeccable self-restraint. Nuclear war has even more ominous dynamics.

The fact is that nobody knows what would happen after the

first tactical nuclear weapon was exploded in combat. General Bernard Rogers, the American military commander of NATO, is among the majority of experts "who believe that the use of theater nuclear weapons would, in fact, escalate to the strategic level, and very quickly."

Even theoreticians such as Henry Kissinger, whose writings in the 1950s helped popularize the notion of limited nuclear war, express skepticism about the chances of keeping nuclear conflicts within predictable bounds. "I originally favored the idea, or the doctrine, of limited nuclear war as a form of deterrence," Kissinger said in a recent interview. "But even after twenty-five years of experience with the idea, nobody has ever produced a model of limited nuclear war I could support or which made any sense."

Thus the basic irony: nuclear weapons—the special crutch that nominally props up NATO's defenses—cannot be used without, in all likelihood, obliterating Europe in the process. The destruction could easily extend to the United States and the Soviet Union as well.

There are practical problems, moreover, in relying on tactical nuclear weapons to repulse a conventional attack. The United States has elaborate command and control arrangements under which the President must authorize the use of nuclear weapons. (As Harry Truman once said, we have never wanted to allow some "dashing Lieutenant Colonel" to make the decision that could start World War III.) In the case of weapons stationed in Europe, we have further arrangements involving consultation with the host country before the devices are used.

However, if there were a sudden Russian attack, and a U.S. base, say, on the border with East Germany were overrun, there would be little time for necessary clearances. Although committed to a first use of nuclear weapons to deal with just such an invasion, we may have something closer to a de facto no-first-use posture. Our military commanders in the field, rather than being able to rely on these weapons, have said that they are scared to death about using them because of the risks of uncontrollable escalation. The unwillingness to use what is, in theory, one of their principal sources of strength, leads to profound confusion about what it is they are supposed to do if a major conflict ever arises.

The lack of a coherent plan for the use of nuclear weapons in the European theater was emphasized after Secretary Alexander Haig testified before Congress in November 1981. He stated that NATO had a plan to fire a "demonstration" nuclear blast—a kind of shot over the bow to warn the Soviets they were going too far. Secretary of Defense Caspar Weinberger said this was not so. When asked, one week later, about a nuclear warning shot, President Reagan, who presumably would have to authorize such a move, said: "There seems to be some confusion as to whether that is still a part of NATO strategy or not, and so far I've had no answer to that."

NATO officials claim that the West benefits from the apparent uncertainty about its plans for using nuclear weapons. As General Rogers observed, "the strategy is deliberately vague about the precise nature of NATO's response to aggression."

The Soviets, in other words, are best kept guessing. The problem, though, is that ambiguous policies keep NATO itself confused about what exactly it should be doing to provide for its own defense.

NATO has dramatically built up its conventional forces over the years to counter the Soviet army. By leaning, however, on the first-use crutch, the Allies have not given this effort the full priority it has deserved. Nor, in assessing the strength of their present nonnuclear defenses, have they given themselves full credit for the capability they have achieved.

A no-first-use policy, in contrast, would clarify NATO's prime military goals and allow it to move away from the threat, less and less credible as time goes on, to engage in limited nuclear war as its main way of stopping Soviet aggression.

After all, what would contribute more to NATO's security than conventional forces that could repulse a Soviet attack without resort to any nuclear weapons? This is what a no-first-use policy would require: a clear firebreak between conventional conflict and nuclear war. An adequate conventional capability, not a knee-jerk use of nuclear weapons, would be the bulwark of NATO's security.

A commitment to maintain adequate conventional forces does not mean that NATO would abandon its nuclear deterrent —give up the ability to retaliate if the U.S.S.R. uses nuclear weapons or goes too far in a conventional war. NATO's nuclear strength would always be there in the background as a sobering factor in Soviet planning, for a policy barring initial use does not preclude possible use. In 1967, NATO shifted from a policy of inevitable nuclear response to that of a possible response without weakening deterrence. A no-first-use policy could similarly be adopted, without jarring consequences, as another step in the evolution of NATO doctrine.

No-first-use, it should be emphasized, is not rhetoric aimed at influencing Soviet behavior. Nor is it merely a high statement of moral principle on the West's commitment not to start a nuclear war. The adoption of such a policy is chiefly intended to provide guidance *within* NATO on what the alliance partners should be doing to maintain and improve their defenses. It would imply a major shift in emphasis in the way troops are trained, forces deployed, and defensive weaponry developed. That is the overriding purpose of adopting such a stance.

Far from being an empty pledge, a no-first-use policy would have dramatic implications, not just on defensive preparations but on the size and make-up of NATO nuclear forces as well. It would become practical under such a policy to remove the NATO tactical nuclear weapons now precariously stationed— in a potential "use or lose" situation—within a few miles of the border between East and West Germany. A further consequence would be the possibility, in time, of bilateral steps to create nuclear-weapons-free zones in Western and Eastern Europe and, ultimately, the removal of all land-based nuclear weapons from European soil. This would leave NATO with a submarine-based deterrent that would give it massive nuclear capability—without the risk that installations on the continent itself would be potential targets of a Soviet first strike.

Thus, unlike the Soviets' no-first-use policy, which they

have exploited for propaganda purposes, a no-first-use policy adopted by NATO would manifest itself in very tangible ways. It would be a military doctrine that guides both the day-to-day work of NATO as well as its crisis planning.

Let nuclear weapons be the ultimate guarantor of NATO's security, but *not* the mainstay of its initial response to Soviet conventional attacks.

21

DEFENDING THE CONTINENT

"Now, as one who spent a lot of time in Europe in peace and war, I'm not too concerned about the Soviet Union and Western Europe. I would think if the Soviet Union attacked Western Europe with conventional forces, they'd have a very, very difficult time of it."
—*General James Gavin, 1981*

THIRTY YEARS AGO, with Western Europe ravaged by World War II, the newly formed NATO alliance lacked the resources to mount a strong conventional defense. The situation has changed over the years, and allied forces have been steadily and dramatically upgraded. Western defenses are now strong enough to counter an invasion and make any attack by the Soviet Union a perilously unattractive proposition. In addition, improvements can be made, at modest cost, that will further strengthen NATO's ability to handle such a contingency.

It is thus feasible, from the point of view of its conventional capability, for NATO to adopt a no-first-use nuclear weapons policy.

In terms of economic and technological prowess, the United States and NATO are far stronger than the Soviet Union and the Warsaw Pact. NATO spends about $300 billion per year on defense, as opposed to about $270 billion for the Pact. With a combined gross domestic product nearly five times greater, NATO can continue to outspend the Pact, if necessary, and can, at any rate, surely afford an adequate defense.

"Europe can be defended by conventional forces provided we take advantage of modern technology, almost a monopoly of the West, and at the same time make certain simple, but profound, reforms," retired Admiral Noel Gayler has said. "This need not involve significant increased expense or manpower—the idea is to do it smart."

In terms of military manpower, the two sides are closely matched. The United States and NATO have about 4.9 million soldiers; the Soviet Union and Warsaw Pact countries have about 4.7 million, not all of which are deployed against the West. China, with whom the Soviet Union shares a long border, has about 4.7 million people in its armed forces, most of whom are positioned against the U.S.S.R. The Soviet Union has to devote about one quarter of its troops to guard against the Chinese threat.

On the Central European front, NATO and Warsaw Pact forces are approximately equal, with little over a million troops on each side. Beyond numerical considerations, there is the additional fact that nearly half of the Warsaw Pact divisions are comprised of Polish and Czech soldiers, who are not considered dependable in the event of a Soviet attack. Western Europeans, it is generally conceded, are more likely to fight for their freedoms than Eastern Europeans are to risk their lives for the U.S.S.R.

In conventional military hardware, as well as in troops, there is an overall balance between NATO and the Warsaw Pact. While the Pact has numerical leads in most offensive weapons, "NATO still retains its overall qualitative edge," according to the Defense Department's *Annual Report* for 1982.

Tanks are primarily offensive weapons intended for invasions. The Warsaw Pact has more of them by a margin of about 2 to 1, but this advantage is offset by NATO's substantial edge in antitank guided missiles. (Recent improvements in this technology are likely to make tanks obsolete very quickly.) These defensive weapons are far more important to NATO than acquiring additional tanks, although its newer ones are generally considered superior in quality to those of the Pact.

The Pact has about twice as many tactical aircraft at its disposal. NATO planes, however, are equipped with advanced radar and Sidewinder missiles and are far more sophisticated. Owing to superior design, they can handle and accelerate better and can also carry a far greater weapons load. Recent evidence of this: during June 1982 skirmishes, Israeli pilots flying U.S.-built F–15 and F–16 fighter jets gunned down Syria's Russian-built MIG–21s and 23s at a ratio of more than 30 to 1.

In terms of naval forces, NATO countries have a definite advantage, both quantitatively and qualitatively. They have more major ships and submarines than the Pact. Their ships are also larger, carrying greater firepower and more sailors.

In short, forces deployed in Europe are roughly equivalent. According to a recent NATO study, the West has the defensive capability to prevent the Warsaw Pact, despite its emphasis on offensive weapons, from gaining a decisive edge. No deficiency in NATO's strength invites a Soviet attack.

There are imbalances between NATO and Warsaw Pact weaponry, the recent NATO report noted, but the Western allies have been taking steps to deal with them. These imbalances have existed for some time without major consequences, for they are neither of a type or magnitude that would give the attacker a compelling advantage.

Take the Soviet lead in tanks, for example. NATO need not match the Pact tank for tank because of the West's lead in precision-guided antitank weaponry, which neutralizes the apparent Soviet advantage. Modern tanks, worth about $2 million, can now be destroyed by missiles that cost less than $10,000.

These and other precision-guided munitions, which are revolutionizing conventional warfare, can be fired from planes, helicopters, and artillery shells. One such weapon, now under development by the United States, is the Assault Breaker. Fitted with 30 to 40 small warheads, it will be able to fend off a whole company of tanks.

New defensive weapons, along with passive devices such as mines, are more practical for use against enemy tanks than either tanks or nuclear explosives. Recent technological advances in antitank weapons have been so great that "many qualified persons believe that before long tanks will be as obsolete as the cavalry," Nobel Prize–winning physicist Hans Bethe recently said.

Rather than building more tanks, NATO should keep doing what it has been doing: concentrating on perfecting antitank weapons. It's not clear what NATO forces would do with greatly increased numbers of tanks anyway, since they have no plans for a blitzkrieg raid on the Eastern bloc.

NATO defenses can be further strengthened by a number of other measures that will cost relatively little. Better planning, training, and communication is needed to ensure a coordinated response among the various armed forces of the Western alliance. This is primarily a matter of organization, not one of hardware.

NATO munitions and precision-guided missiles stored near the Central Front would last less than 30 days in a major conflict. NATO defenses could be substantially upgraded by increased "prepositioning" of supplies—that is, by storing more tanks, ammunition, missiles, and spare parts in key European locations. This could be done for less than $10 billion and could be paid in one year as part of the increase in defense spending already agreed to by NATO countries.

One of the most effective and inexpensive ways to stave off a Soviet tank invasion—which is a primary concern among the NATO allies—would be to dig ditches, erect barriers, and prepare defenses along expected invasion routes. The Israelis, for example, have dug ditches between Syria and the Golan Heights and also built concrete "tank traps" to block the advance of Syrian tanks. In addition, the Israelis have set up ramps and other obstacles to protect their own tanks.

NATO, however, has made little effort to place obstacles

at pivotal points along its eastern border where a tank attack is possible. This reluctance is difficult to explain, for such a simple measure might, in fact, be the best and cheapest insurance policy Europe could buy.

In nuclear warfare, no defenses have proved feasible. In conventional warfare, in contrast, technology has been increasing the odds in favor of the defense. Yesterday's awesome battleships and tanks are today's sitting ducks. With its strong emphasis on exploiting the new technological possibilities, NATO holds advantages that effectively blunt the offensive capabilities of the Warsaw Pact. The Pact is deprived of the overwhelming offensive edge considered necessary for a successful breakthrough attack.

No weakness in NATO's conventional forces, therefore, would encourage the Soviet Union to take the incredible risk of beginning a war that—no-first-use policies aside—it knows might escalate into World War III.

22

THE NEW ARMY

"There is no way, as long as Saudi Arabia and the OPEC nations there in the [Mid-East] . . . provide the bulk of the energy that is needed to turn the wheels of industry in the Western world . . . that we could stand by and see that taken over by anyone that would shut off that oil."
—*President Reagan,*
October 1, 1981

PROTECTING the West's access to vital Persian Gulf oil sup-plies ranks just below protecting North America and Western Europe as a U.S. defense priority. To this end, the United States is building a Rapid Deployment Force (RDF) that will allow it to "project power" into the region.

Alarm about the potential Soviet threat to the Persian Gulf was heightened by CIA reports in the late 1970s which con-cluded that the Russians were running out of oil. The overly pessimistic estimates of the Soviet Union's domestic oil reserves were later revised, but worries about Soviet designs on the region persist.

When the Soviets invaded Afghanistan in December 1979, there was immediate speculation that this was a prelude to an attack on the Persian Gulf. President Carter promptly declared that U.S. policy would be to fight "by any means necessary" to safeguard the West's access to Mideast oil, an announcement widely interpreted as a veiled threat to use nuclear weapons.

It is a mistake, however, to regard the Middle East oil problem in purely military terms. Over the long run, there is an obvious nonmilitary alternative for the West: a full-scale effort to avoid the shock of an oil cutoff by reducing dependence on the region's oil.

The West could accomplish this, in principle, by diversifying its energy supplies, stockpiling oil, and by a comprehensive energy conservation program that reduced oil imports from this unstable region. The new army that could accomplish these goals would consist not of soldiers but of scientists, engineers, carpenters, and others assigned to alternate energy programs and energy conservation efforts. None of these nonmilitary initiatives would be easy. They would probably be less difficult, less expensive, and less risky, than the creation of a multibillion-dollar Rapid Deployment Force that, somehow, is supposed to be able to defend that distant region.

According to current plans, the United States will spend $4 billion in 1983 and about $20 billion over the next five years to build up, train, and provide air and sea transport for an RDF capable of fighting in the Mideast. This is part of a broader strategy to prepare U.S. forces to intervene around the globe at any time and any place. "Like it or not, the U.S. is now the point man in the world," Army Chief of Staff General Edward Meyer has explained.

There is nothing new about this strategy. The United States already has the capability to send combat troops—the Marines —around the globe, and it is not clear that a Rapid Deployment Force could deal with Soviet aggression any better than existing forces.

A major problem is logistical. Most countries in the Middle East—even allies such as Egypt—are opposed to having U.S. troops stationed on their soil. Saudi leaders are particularly worried that a large U.S. presence could lead to domestic turmoil. They also fear that U.S. troops might be used against *them* in an oil crisis. "We don't want your RDF," a Saudi military official told Secretary Weinberger.

Arab apprehension increased when the Department of Defense spelled out what the United States included in its policy of using "any means necessary" to defend the region. To prevail, the Pentagon said, the U.S. "might have to threaten or make use of tactical nuclear weapons."

This is no idle threat. All major U.S. military forces, from European-based troops to the Pacific fleet, are equipped with and trained to use nuclear weapons. Following a Soviet invasion or threatened invasion of the Gulf, U.S. troops could, indeed, swiftly bring these weapons to the region.

What the United States would do next, however, remains an unanswered question, for it is difficult to see how nuclear weapons can be used without jeopardizing the oil we're trying to protect. The flow of oil depends on a fragile complex of wells, pumping stations, and pipelines. The Soviets might seize these facilities, but America would surely not want to counterattack with nuclear devices. This could well lead to World War III, the local damage notwithstanding.

In fact, it is doubtful that any degree of military strength—nuclear or otherwise—can guarantee protection of exceedingly vulnerable oil supplies. The conventional forces that the United States has helped its allies in the region to maintain may, to some extent, help discourage potential aggressors. The fear that an outright takeover might prompt drastic U.S. actions also serves to deter Soviet adventurism in the region.

In the final analysis, though, we must recognize that an expanded military capability in the region will not assure a continued flow of oil. This reality must be reflected in the long-term strategy the West adopts to reduce its dangerous dependence on the region.

The United States is much less reliant on Mideast oil than its Western European allies. It accounts for only about 10 percent of the oil we use, about 5 percent of the total energy use. Western Europe, in contrast, gets about 44 percent of its oil from the region or about 23 percent of its total fuel requirements.

This is not the place for a detailed review of the world energy problem. From the extensive studies on this subject, however, it is clear that there are far-reaching possibilities for continued improvements in energy efficiency. These measures would dramatically reduce fuel requirements and hence the need for dependence on Mideast oil.

Over the longer run, the development of alternate energy sources, such as solar energy—which cannot be embargoed by the Arabs or cut off by the Soviets—would also contribute to this goal. The United States and its allies must pursue these opportunities aggressively.

For less money than it plans to spend over the next five years on the RDF and on continued oil imports from the Middle East, for example, the United States could "weatherize" and insulate 25 million homes. It could also subsidize the replacement of 45 million automobiles with more efficient ones. The total savings from such a program would be about 2 million barrels of oil per day—which is more than the country currently imports from the Mideast.

Thus, rather than readying troops to fight for oil in remote deserts, we would do far better to employ a new army of construction workers and engineers to install energy-saving technology in America's homes, cars, and factories.

Europe and Japan, who are even more dependent on imported oil, would do well to follow our example.

23

COMING UP FOR AIR

"More than any other time in history, mankind now faces a crossroads. One path leads to despair and utter hopelessness. The other, to total extinction. Let us pray we have the wisdom to choose correctly."

—Woody Allen, 1979

HISTORY, Gibbon wrote in *The Decline and Fall of the Roman Empire,* is "little more than the register of the crimes, follies, and misfortunes of mankind." He was tallying human miseries that are far less gruesome than those that have become possible in more recent times.

The present century, before it was half over, had seen two world wars, numerous lesser ones, barbaric genocide, the rise of maniacal leaders, and the emergence of powerful totalitarian states.

As if the tide against humankind were not strong enough, the second half of the century has witnessed a relentless buildup of exterminating weaponry whose potential ill effects dwarf all the calamities in man's troubled past. As trauma follows trauma, a sanguine view of the prospects for human survival becomes difficult to sustain.

Still, in the current, worldwide efforts to oppose the nuclear arms race lies a basis for guarded optimism. The threat of annihilation, at least, has been recognized; the steps that are needed to reduce it are beginning to be discussed; the possibility that nuclear war can be avoided still exists.

Thus, instead of choosing between Woody Allen's two roads to oblivion, there is growing resolve to forge a new road. No one can pretend that it will lead to the promised land. All we can hope is that it will lead away from nuclear war.

The threat of nuclear holocaust has been a fact of life for so long that it seems naive to contemplate plans the United States and U.S.S.R. can make once that danger recedes. Yet it may be the attractiveness of those plans that convinces the two superpowers of the need to abandon the costly arms race, for both the dream of affluence in the capitalist United States and the promise of a socialist utopia in the U.S.S.R. are in great jeopardy. Both countries are beset by grave domestic problems that are growing all the worse because of the massive drain on their resources for military purposes.

In the United States, the accumulating economic troubles of the past decade have created fundamental doubts about the country's future material well-being. Chronic inflation and unemployment are the most evident signs of the country's shaky prosperity. Declining productivity, slackening technological progress, and an inability to keep up with Japanese and European competition are further indicators of weakness in the once-booming American economy.

Lavish military programs, which siphon critical scientific and engineering personnel away from America's civilian industries, have been a significant factor in the economic decline. About a third of the technical talent in the United States has been employed over the last twenty-five years in military-related work. This is a major sacrifice for an economic system whose growth and revitalization depends on its ability to exploit advanced technology.

Every innovation in weaponry is achieved at the expense of gains in civilian industries. Instead of refining missile guidance systems, the scientists and engineers *could* be developing new energy technology, new methods to improve manufacturing productivity, new products for international markets. Our major international rival, Japan, is not shackled by a costly obsession with military gadgetry, having abandoned the militaristic policies that led it to World War II.

The Soviet economy, much less efficient and productive than ours, yet required to support a larger population, has suffered correspondingly from the costs of frenzied military programs. Its faltering agricultural sector, backward electronics industry, and chronic inability to provide adequate supplies of basic consumer goods create urgent difficulties. Not the least of Soviet worries was demonstrated in Poland when widespread protest against shortages of food, rising prices, and falling wages prompted near revolution. If this type of fundamental challenge to the Soviet system is ignored, and the civilian economy allowed to languish and decay, the very existence of the Soviet state will be threatened.

Thus, if avoiding the dangers of nuclear war were not, in itself, a sufficiently compelling goal, there are concrete economic incentives that encourage the two superpowers to curb their insatiable military appetites.

Although freed from an all-consuming military rivalry, the two nations would not expect to become the best of friends, but they might still see the merits of joint programs that would help them achieve common goals.

Both superpowers would benefit from a halt in the spread of nuclear weapons around the globe. Owing to the wide availability of nuclear materials as well as access to the knowledge of how to fashion nuclear bombs, the danger of proliferation is acute. A cooperative U.S.-U.S.S.R. effort to provide other nations assistance in their commercial nuclear programs, while simultaneously tightening safeguards on nuclear fuel and technology, might help stem this frightening development. Their own good example in foregoing further nuclear weapons acquisitions would be the first step in trying to curb the potential nuclear ambitions of other countries.

Both nations would ultimately gain if they terminated the ill-considered alliances they have pursued for vague cold war objectives. Their game of propping up unsavory regimes, in countries where they have no interest apart from upstaging the other, might profitably be abandoned.

The superpowers will suffer in the long run if the Third World, under the pressure of population growth and a desperate scramble for resources, devolves into seething turmoil. Advanced weapons costing billions of dollars are exported by the United States and U.S.S.R. to these nations, serving little purpose other than to elevate the level of violence that could be inflicted in local conflicts. The two nations, in concert with the other major arms suppliers, should begin to take steps to restrain the indiscriminate dispensation of lethal military hardware.

If the two nations do, indeed, halt the nuclear arms race, after a generation of ferocious, nonstop competition, they will finally be able to come up for air. It will be refreshing for both nations to have the opportunity to decide, with the appalling specter of nuclear fire storms no longer looming so closely above them, exactly what objectives they should pursue.

One can hope they will find ends that will contribute more to their future than the nuclear weapons stockpiles that are each country's current legacy to its children.

NOTES

INTRODUCTION: NUCLEAR ANGST (pages ix–xi)

ix   "To the village square."   Albert Einstein, "The Real Problem is in the Hearts of Men," *New York Times Magazine*, June 23, 1946.

xi   "freeze the United States into a position."   Bernard Gwertzman, "State Dept. Calls Arms Freeze Plan 'Dangerous' To U.S." *New York Times*, March 12, 1982.

PART I: THE NUCLEAR ARMS RACE

1. A WARNING (pages 3–4)

3   "It's a damn shame."   "Tempers High Near Blast Site," *Arkansas Gazette*, September 21, 1980.

3   "I'm no nuclear physicist."   Daniel Ford, "The Accident," *The New Yorker*, October 6, 1980.

3   "We're surrounded."   Ford.

4   "I never thought much."   Francis Clines, "Fright Turns to Anger in Arkansas Hamlet," *New York Times*, September 20, 1980.

4   "We want the blooming things."   Ford.

4   "I wasn't aware."   Ford.

4   "I really work very hard."   Ford.

4   "I don't want Russia."   Ford.

2. THE BALANCE SHEET (pages 5–12)

5   "The number of tactical nuclear weapons?"   Center for Defense Information, telephone conversation, June 7, 1982.

7   "First we need enough Minutemen."   Solly Zuckerman, *Nuclear Illusion and Reality* (New York: Viking, 1982), p. 46.

11   "We're way ahead."   Paul Warnke. "Which Comes First, Arms Control or Security?" *New York Times*, March 21, 1982.

11   "What in the name of God?"   R. Jeffrey Smith, "They Have More EMT Than We," *Science*, Vol. 216, April 1982, p. 32.

3. MUTUAL SUSPICION (pages 13–15)

13 "It may seem." Richard Nixon, "America Has Slipped To Number Two," *Parade,* October 5, 1980, p. 7.

13 "God almighty." John L. Gaddis, *The United States and the Origins of the Cold War* (New York: Columbia University Press, 1972), p. 245.

14 "Our monopoly of the bomb." Daniel Yergin, *Shattered Peace* (Boston: Houghton Mifflin, 1977), p. 265.

14 "We cannot at this time." Yergin.

14 "the war isn't over." Gaddis, p. 350.

15 "My own theory." Francis FitzGerald, "The Reverend Jerry Falwell," *The New Yorker,* May 18, 1981, pp. 130–31.

15 "This political force." George Kennan, "The Long Telegram." February 22, 1946.

15 "I think it is a mistake." Yergin, p. 275.

4. THE CAUCUS RACE (pages 16–20)

16 "Senator Brooke... Admiral Moorer." *Authorization for Military Procurement Research and Development, FY 1970,* Hearings before the Committee on Armed Services, U.S. Senate, 91st Congress (Washington, D.C.: U.S. Government Printing Office, March 19, 1969), p. 673.

17 "scare hell out of the country." Tom Gervasi, *Arsenal of Democracy II* (New York: Grove Press, 1981), p. 20.

18 "What I read." Daniel Yergin, *Shattered Peace* (Boston: Houghton Mifflin, 1977), p. 403.

19 "In three years." Stuart Symington, *New York Times,* March 16, 1959.

19 "At this point." James R. Shepley, "Life and Death Over the Missile Program," *Life,* March 9, 1959.

20 "a 1001 technical delights." R. Jeffrey Smith, "Trucks, Trenches, Trains, and Blimps," *Science,* Vol. 216, April 9, 1982, p. 153.

5. TO THE BRINK (pages 21–23)

21 "A missile is a missile." James A. Nathan, "The Tragic Enshrinement of Toughness," *Major Problems in American Foreign Policy,* edited by Thomas G. Paterson (Lexington, Mass.: D.C. Heath, 1978), p. 431.

21 "the armaments and military equipment." President John F. Kennedy, television address, October 22, 1962.

22 "It is generally agreed." Theodore Sorensen, "Memorandum on Executive Committee Discussions," October 17, 1962.

22 "but the Administration certainly was." Richard Barnet, *The Giants: Russians and Americans* (New York: Simon & Schuster, 1977), p. 60.

22 "Nobody in the White House." Nathan, p. 434.

23 "If you hadn't acted." Barnet, p. 60.

23 "Kennedy might be playing." Nathan, p. 431.

23 "were on the edge." Nathan, p. 428.

6. A (VERY) LIMITED TEST BAN (pages 24–26)

24 "One of the political prices." Herbert York, *Race to Oblivion* (New York: Simon & Schuster, 1970), p. 45.

25 "The real reason." Solly Zuckerman. *Nuclear Illusion and Reality* (New York: Viking, 1982).

25 "When I saw the details." Joseph Nye, "Test Ban Treaty," *New York Times Book Review*, February 28, 1982, p. 27.

26 "We learned that with a little ingenuity." Elizabeth Drew, "An Argument over Survival," *The New Yorker*, April 4, 1977, p. 100.

7. RULES OF THE GAME (pages 27–32)

27 "Rather than slowing." Richard Burt, "Limited Ceiling," *New York Times*, December 24, 1978.

29 "If we have to start over again." "MX Plan," *Boston Globe*, October 4, 1981.

30 "I didn't realize the Pentagon." Elizabeth Drew, "An Argument over Survival," *The New Yorker*, April 4, 1977, p. 103.

31 "This was the theory behind SALT I." *Military Implications of the Treaty on the Limitation of Strategic Offensive Arms and Protocol Thereto (SALT II Treaty)*, Hearings before the Committee on Armed Services, U.S. Senate, 95th Congress, Part 2 (Washington, D.C.: U.S. Government Printing Office, 1979), p. 869.

32 "Arms control negotiations." Richard Barnet. *The Giants: Russians and Americans* (New York: Simon & Schuster, 1977), p. 102.

32 "I wish I had thought through the implications." Drew, p. 102.

8. THE EXTRAVAGANCE GAP (pages 33–37)

33 "If we don't spend enough." Richard Nixon, ABC Television interview, May 8, 1980.

35 "without precedent in history." Bernard Brodie, "Development of Nuclear Strategy," *International Security*, Vol. 2, No. 4, Spring 1978.

35 "reminiscent of Nazi Germany's." Committee on the Present Danger, "What is the Soviet Union Up To?" Washington, D.C., 1977.

36 "I don't think it's fair." Committee on the Present Danger, "Peace with Freedom," Washington, D.C., 1978.

37 "By computing Soviet manpower costs." Richard Barnet, *The Giants: Russians and Americans* (New York: Simon & Schuster, 1977), p. 52.

37 "It is time that the American public." Senator William Proxmire, *Congressional Record*, August 26, 1980.

9. THE MYTH OF VULNERABILITY (pages 38–43)

38 "The Soviets don't have to pull the trigger." R. Jeffrey Smith, "An Upheaval in U.S. Strategic Thought," *Science*, Vol. 216, April 2, 1982, p. 33.

38 "affect the Soviet perception."   Joint Chiefs of Staff, *Military Posture For FY 1980* (Washington, D.C.: U.S. Government Printing Office, 1979).

39 "The real risk."   Eugene Rostow, "Which Comes First, Arms Control or Security?" *New York Times,* March 21, 1982.

39 "a game of chess."   Paul Nitze, "Atoms, Strategy, and Policy," *Foreign Affairs,* January 1956, pp. 187–198.

40 "I have always found."   CBS News, "The Defense of the United States," June 14, 1981.

41 "It's something we will never."   CBS News, "The Defense of the United States."

41 "do not have an acceptable PK."   Christopher Paine, "Running in circles with the MX," *The Bulletin of the Atomic Scientists,* December 1981, p. 6.

42 "Nothing has been put forward."   John Newhouse, "Arms and Orthodoxy," *The New Yorker,* June 7, 1982, p. 89.

42 "They would deter anyone."   Harold Brown, *New York Times,* September 21, 1980.

42 "there is really no reason."   Richard Garwin, "Future Strategic Forces," Paper presented at the International Seminar on the World-Wide Implications of a Nuclear War, Erice-Trapani, Sicily, August 18, 1981.

43 "We've done stupid things before."   ABC News, "The Apocalypse Game," April 24, 1981.

10. THE IMPOTENCE COMPLEX (pages 44–46)

44 "It is time to wake up."   Richard Nixon, "America Has Slipped to Number Two," *Parade,* October 5, 1980, pp. 7, 9.

45 "What do you expect?"   Marvin Harris, *America Now* (New York: Simon & Schuster, 1981), p. 18.

45 "To a certain extent."   R. Jeffrey Smith, "An Upheaval in U.S. Strategic Thought," *Science,* Vol. 216, April 2, 1982, p. 33.

46 "The Russians could walk right in."   Frances FitzGerald, "The Reverend Jerry Falwell," *The New Yorker,* May 18, 1981, p. 132.

46 "It is time for us to start."   CBS News, "The Defense of the United States," June 14, 1981.

PART II: THE NEW BUILDUP

11. MORE OF EVERYTHING (pages 49–55)

49 "We never articulated."   Flora Lewis, "Dispute and Drift," *New York Times,* February 21, 1982.

49 "We need everything."   Michael Heylin, "Nuclear arms race gearing for speedup," *Chemical and Engineering News,* March 16, 1981, p. 28.

49 "got a blank check."   William Greider, "The Education of David Stockman," *The Atlantic Monthly,* December 1981, p. 43.

50 "will signal our resolve."   Robert Cooke, "It's a never-ending search for the best," *Boston Globe,* April 4, 1982.

50 "would be a dangerous and misleading signal." R. Jeffrey Smith, "Reagan's Plan For MX Attracts Fire," *Science*, Vol. 216, April 9, 1982, p. 152.

51 "I think we ought to look." R. Jeffrey Smith, "A Doomsday Plan for the 1990s," *Science*, Vol. 216, April 23, 1982, p. 389.

52 "This whole MX thing." Benjamin Taylor, "Senate rejects Reagan's MX silo plan," *Boston Globe*, December 3, 1981.

52 "$40 Billion flying Edsel." "Cost of 100 B-1 Bombers Figured at Double AF Estimate," *New York Times*, November 10, 1981.

53 "fact that its one mission." "Reagan stands by nuclear fight remarks," *Boston Globe*, November 11, 1981.

53 "until 1990." Richard Halloran, "Weinberger and the Press: Point, Counterpoint," *New York Times*, March 4, 1982.

53 "Does the U.S. need to buy?" Michael Johnson, "Debunking the Window of Vulnerability," *Technology Review*, January 1982, p. 61.

54 "Take the number of nuclear subs." Hyman Rickover, "Excerpts from Farewell Testimony by Rickover to Congress," *New York Times*, January 30, 1982.

54 "If you know anything." Gary Reich, "Taking Aim," *Barron's*, March 22, 1982, p. 8.

54 "tremendous symbolic value." John Warner, "Debate: Can 1940's Ship Play a Useful Part in the 1980's Navy?," *New York Times*, December 20, 1981.

55 "To paraphrase Will Rogers." Les Aspin, "Bigger Bucks For Security—But How Much and For What?" *New York Times*, March 14, 1982.

55 "They didn't go into the process." U.S. Defense Policy: The Right Direction?" *U.S. News & World Report*, November 23, 1981, p. 25.

12. FIRST STRIKE (pages 56–62)

56 "We in the military." Dave Meyers, "The Last Europe," *The Bulletin of the Atomic Scientists*, March 1982, p. 23.

57 "smoking radiation ruin." "U.S. in '50s Had Plan for Strike on Soviets," *Washington Post*, February 15, 1982.

57 "that if the U.S. is pushed." *Washington Post*, February 15, 1982.

57 "It has become clear." Robert Scheer, "Fear of a U.S. First Strike Seen as Cause of Arms Race," *Los Angeles Times*, April 8, 1982.

58 "render ineffective." Richard Halloran, "Pentagon Draws Up First Strategy for Fighting a Long Nuclear War," *New York Times*, May 30, 1982.

58 "prevail and be able to force." Fred Kaplan, "Nuclear War Strategy Not New—or Practical," *Boston Globe*, June 13, 1982.

58 "will convince the Soviets." Tom Wicker, "A Switch for the MX," *New York Times*, February 19, 1982.

59 "It has proved difficult." R. Jeffrey Smith, "Pentagon Moves Toward First Strike Capability," *Science*, Vol. 215, May 7, 1982, p. 596.

59 "preemptive capability." Associated Press, October 14, 1981.

60 "The niceties of targeting doctrine." McGeorge Bundy, "Strategic

deterrence after 30 years," Keynote remarks at the Annual Conference of the International Institute for Strategic Studies, Villars, Switzerland.

60   "enormous" and "uncertainties are such that." Office of Technology Assessment, "The Effects of Nuclear War," U.S. Congress, Washington, D.C., 1979.

60   "Real war is not like." Noel Gayler, "How to Break the Momentum of the Arms Race," *New York Times Magazine,* April 25, 1982, p. 48.

61   "We have to target." James Lardner, "The Call of the Hawk's Hawk," *Washington Post,* May 14, 1982.

61   "Is it sensible?" Colin Gray and Keith Payne, "Victory Is Possible," *Foreign Policy,* No. 39, Summer 1980, p. 24.

61   "you can have a winner." Robert Scheer, interview with George Bush, *Los Angeles Times,* January 23, 1980.

61   "Think tank analysts." R. Jeffrey Smith, "An Upheaval in U.S. Strategic Thought," *Science,* Vol. 216, April 2, 1982, p. 32.

62   "If we use our 10,000 warheads." Paul Warnke, "Which Comes First, Arms Control or Security?" *New York Times,* March 21, 1982.

62   "What many Americans do not understand." Gayler, "How to Break the Momentum of the Arms Race," p. 48.

62   "What really deters the Soviet Union." Michael Heylin, "Richard Garwin: arms race's seminal thinker," *Chemical and Engineering News,* September 28, 1981, p. 35.

13. DUCK AND COVER (pages 63–66)

63   "Americans are doers." Natalie Angier, "Can You Survive World War III?," *Parade,* April 4, 1982.

63   "the U.S. could survive." Robert Scheer, "Nuclear war the end?," *Boston Globe,* January 18, 1982, p. 8.

63   "Americans would not be helpless." Scheer, p. 8.

63   "Everybody's going to make it." Robert Scheer, interview with T. K. Jones, *Los Angeles Times,* January 16, 1982.

64   "Color what you would need." Bernard Weinraub, "Civil Defense Agency: 'Trying to Do Something,' " *New York Times,* April 8, 1982.

64   "Deceased, Mortuary No. 10." Weinraub.

65   "whether you want to be." Angier.

66   "Comrade, what should we do?" John F. Burns, "Russians, Too, Joke Sadly on Atom-War Survival," *New York Times,* June 11, 1982.

66   "grob." Burns.

66   "extremely dangerous nonsense." Mary Battiata, "In Case of Nuclear War," *Washington Post,* April 24, 1982.

14. THE HIGH GROUND (pages 67–70)

67   "Space is a dandy arena." John Markoff, "Military Needs Encroaching on NASA and Space Shuttle Program," *In These Times,* October 26, 1977.

67 "ground basket." William J. Broad, "A Poor Start for the Militarization of Space," *Science,* Vol. 216, May 7, 1982, p. 605.

67 "a vigorous and comprehensive." George C. Wilson, "U.S. Eyes Lengthy A-War," *Washington Post,* October 5, 1981.

68 "Soviet interceptor satellites." Robert Aldrich, *The Counterforce Syndrome* (Washington, D.C.: Institute for Policy Studies, 1977), p. 18.

68 "The laws of physics." "Soviet Energy Ray a Hoax?" *Boston Globe,* June 2, 1977.

68 "We expect a large." George C. Wilson, "Soviets reported gaining in space weapons," *Boston Globe,* March 3, 1982.

68 "It is nonsense." Associated Press, "Some Scientists Dispute Report on Soviet Laser," *Washington Post,* May 5, 1982.

69 "I think we could." Bernard Weinraub, "Expert Says Soviets May Loft Laser Gun But Doubts Effect," *New York Times,* April 23, 1982.

69 "little fellow travelers." Richard Garwin, NBC "Today" show, March 15, 1982.

15. A FLY IN OUTER SPACE (pages 71–74)

71 "A defensive policy." Michael Heylin, "Richard Garwin: arms race's seminal thinker," *Chemical and Engineering News,* September 28, 1981, p. 25.

71 "We are not yet sure." Fred Kaplan, " '83 Budget and MX," *Boston Globe,* February 9, 1982.

72 "a screen of, say, cavalry." Lieutenant General Daniel Graham, NBC "Today" show, March 15, 1982.

72 "given the advances." Jack Ruina, "Where Do We Stand in ABM Technology?," Council for a Livable World, June 1981, p. 1.

72 "a science fiction idea." Phillip M. Boffey, "Laser Weapons: Renewed Focus Raises Fears and Doubts," *New York Times,* March 9, 1982.

73 "The history of BMD development." Richard L. Garwin, "Ballistic Missile Defense (BMD): Silos and Space," IBM Thomas J. Watson Research Center, February 5, 1982, p. 1.

73 "won't work." Richard L. Garwin, "Ballistic Missile Defenses in the 1980's?" Council for a Livable World, June 1981, p. 1.

16. LIGHTING FUSES (pages 75–79)

75 "Missiles will bring." Omar N. Bradley, speech at St. Alban's School, Washington, D.C., November 5, 1957.

75 "Too often our technologists say." Tom Buckley, "A Voice of Reason Among Nuclear Warriors," *Quest,* March 1981, p. 84.

76 "the U.S. is racing with itself." Jerome Wiesner, talk at the University of Chicago, November 11, 1981.

76 "If we go ahead." Paul Warnke, "Which Comes First, Arms Control or Security?" *New York Times,* March 21, 1982.

77 "The Soviet Union is fully resolved." Henry Trofimenko, "Coun-

terforce: Illusion of a Panacea," *International Security,* Vol. 5, No. 4, Spring 1981, p. 28.

78   "What we're trying to do."   R. Jeffrey Smith, "Pentagon Moves Toward First-Strike Capability," *Science,* Vol. 216, May 7, 1982, p. 597.

78   "The U.S.S.R. can't match the U.S."   Smith.

78   "We know we're not."   "A Complex of Tricky Issues," *Newsweek,* April 26, 1982, p. 26.

78   "I have no doubt."   Robert Scheer, "Fear of a U.S. First Strike Seen as Cause of Arms Race," *Los Angeles Times,* April 8, 1982.

PART III: THE WAY OUT

17. THE SEARCH FOR SOLUTIONS (pages 83–88)

83   "The unleashed power."   Ralph Lapp, "The Letter That Started It All," *New York Times Magazine,* August 2, 1964.

87   "So far as nuclear war."   Roger Fisher, "Can We Negotiate With the Russians?," transcript from Conference on Nuclear Arms Control at the First Parish Church in Weston, Massachusetts, November 14, 1981.

18. ENDGAME (pages 89–93)

89   "People want."   Dwight Eisenhower, *London Sunday Times,* 1960.

90   "a comprehensive ally."   Bernard W. Rogers. "The Atlantic Alliance." *Foreign Affairs,* Vol. 60, No. 5, Summer 1982, p. 1147.

92   "give us."   Daniel P. Moynihan. "Trust Isn't the Issue in Arms Reduction," *New York Times,* May 10, 1982.

92   "in each case."   U.S. Department of State, "SALT and American Security: Questions Americans Are Asking" (Washington, D.C.: Government Printing Office, November 1979).

92   "Since a freeze."   Herbert Scoville, Jr., testimony before the Senate Foreign Relations Committee, May 13, 1982.

93   "I am convinced."   Averell Harriman, Foreword to *Freeze!* by Senator Edward Kennedy and Senator Mark Hatfield (New York: Bantam, 1982), p. xiv.

93   "With every delay."   Solly Zuckerman, *Nuclear Illusion and Reality,* (New York: Viking, 1982), p. 134.

19. WINDING DOWN (pages 94–98)

94   "Is it possible?"   George Kennan, address on the occasion of receiving the Albert Einstein Peace Prize, Washington, D.C., May 19, 1981.

96   "The genie."   Vice Admiral John Marshall Lee, talk at Cornell University, November 11, 1981.

96   "the fact of strongly diminishing."   Alaine Enthoven and K. Wayne Smith, *How Much Is Enough?* (New York: Harper & Row, 1971), p. 207.

97   "without further."   Kennan.

20. NO FIRST USE (pages 99–106)

99 "When they talk." Ronald Steel, "Anti-nuclear protests vs. NATO," *Boston Sunday Globe,* November 8, 1981.

102 "Forces seen on land." "A Debate—Does NATO Really Need Those Missiles?," *New York Times,* November 22, 1981.

102 "one that blows up in Europe." "Which Comes First, Arms Control or Security?," *New York Times,* March 21, 1982.

103 "who believe that the use." "NATO Chief Warns on Nuclear Strategy Debate," *Boston Sunday Globe,* November 8, 1981.

103 "I originally favored the idea." John Newhouse, "Arms and Orthodoxy," *The New Yorker,* June 7, 1982, p. 96.

104 "There seems to be some confusion." President Ronald Reagan, press conference, Washington, D.C., November 10, 1981.

104 "the strategy is deliberately vague." Bernard W. Rogers, "The Atlantic Alliance," *Foreign Affairs,* Vol. 60, No. 5, Summer 1982, p. 1150.

21. DEFENDING THE CONTINENT (pages 107–111)

107 "Now, as one who spent." General James Gavin, speech at Harvard University, November 11, 1981.

108 "Europe can be defended." Admiral Noel Gayler, "News Release," Union of Concerned Scientists, April 7, 1982.

108 "NATO still retains." Department of Defense, *Annual Report to Congress* (Fiscal Year 1982) (Washington, D.C.: Government Printing Office, 1981), p. 75.

110 "many qualified persons." Tom Wicker, "Anti-tank and Antinuke," *New York Times,* April 20, 1982.

22. THE NEW ARMY (pages 112–115)

112 "There is no way." President Reagan, press conference, Washington, D.C., October 1, 1981.

112 "by any means necessary." President Jimmy Carter, State of the Union Address, January 1980.

113 "Like it or not." Center for Defense Information, "The New Military Budget," *The Defense Monitor,* Vol. IX, No. 3, April 1980.

114 "We don't want your RDF." Richard Halloran, "Saudis Say Differences Mar Talks with Weinberger," *New York Times,* February 9, 1982.

114 "might have to threaten." Jonathan Schell, "The Fate of the Earth," *The New Yorker,* February 1, 1982, p. 66.

23. COMING UP FOR AIR (pages 116–119)

116 "More than any other time." Woody Allen. "My Speech to the Graduates," *Side Effects* (New York: Ballantine, 1981), p. 81.

INDEX

ABOUT THE AUTHORS

Daniel Ford, Henry Kendall, and Steven Nadis have worked on a variety of studies under the auspices of the Union of Concerned Scientists. The Cambridge, Massachusetts–based coalition of scientists, engineers, and other professionals focuses on the impact of advanced technology on society and has worked extensively on nuclear energy, environmental issues, and national defense policy.

Daniel Ford, the former Executive Director of UCS, is an economist and writer specializing in nuclear policy questions. His most recent books are *The Cult of the Atom* and *Three Mile Island: Thirty Minutes to Meltdown*. He also writes for *The New Yorker*. Henry Kendall, the Chairman of UCS, is a high-energy experimental physicist and a Professor of Physics at the Massachusetts Institute of Technology. His recent book, *Energy Strategies: Toward a Solar Future,* written with UCS staff writer Steven Nadis, was named one of the year's best books on energy by *Library Journal*.